THE Real Rosalind

THE Real Rosalind

The Truth About Rosalind Franklin's DNA Discovery and How It Was Erased

DEBBIE LOREN DUNN AND JANET FOX

Zest Books™
An imprint of Lerner Publishing Group, Inc.
241 First Avenue North
Minneapolis, MN 55401 USA

For reading levels and more information, look up this title at www.lernerbooks.com.
Visit us at zestbooks.net.

Designed by Athena Currier

Main body text set in Janson Text LT Std.
Typeface provided by Adobe Systems.

Library of Congress Cataloging-in-Publication Data

Names: Dunn, Debbie Loren author | Fox, Janet S. author
Title: The real Rosalind : the truth about Rosalind Franklin's DNA discovery and how it was erased / by Debbie Loren Dunn & Janet Fox.
Description: Minneapolis : Zest Books, [2026] | Includes bibliographical references and index. | Audience: Grades 10–12 | Summary: "The story of British scientist Rosalind Franklin, whose breakthrough discoveries in the field of DNA changed science as we know it, only to have the credit stolen by her male colleagues"— Provided by publisher.
Identifiers: LCCN 2025024642 (print) | LCCN 2025024643 (ebook) | ISBN 9798765627693 library binding | ISBN 9798765627709 paperback | ISBN 9798765659687 epub
Subjects: LCSH: Franklin, Rosalind, 1920–1958 | Chemists—England—Biography | Women chemists—England—Biography | Discoveries in science | Sex discrimination in science—England—History—20th century | LCGFT: Biographies
Classification: LCC QP26.F68 D86 2026 (print) | LCC QP26.F68 (ebook) | DDC 540.92 [B]—dc23/eng/20250813

LC record available at https://lccn.loc.gov/2025024642
LC ebook record available at https://lccn.loc.gov/2025024643

Manufactured in the United States of America
1-1012835-52144-10/2/2025

To David, Sydney, and Abbie —D.L.D.

To Jeff and Kevin, my inspiration in everything —J.F.

Contents

Part 3 Era of Tobacco Mosaic Virus 135

Part 4 The Story Doesn't End Here 183

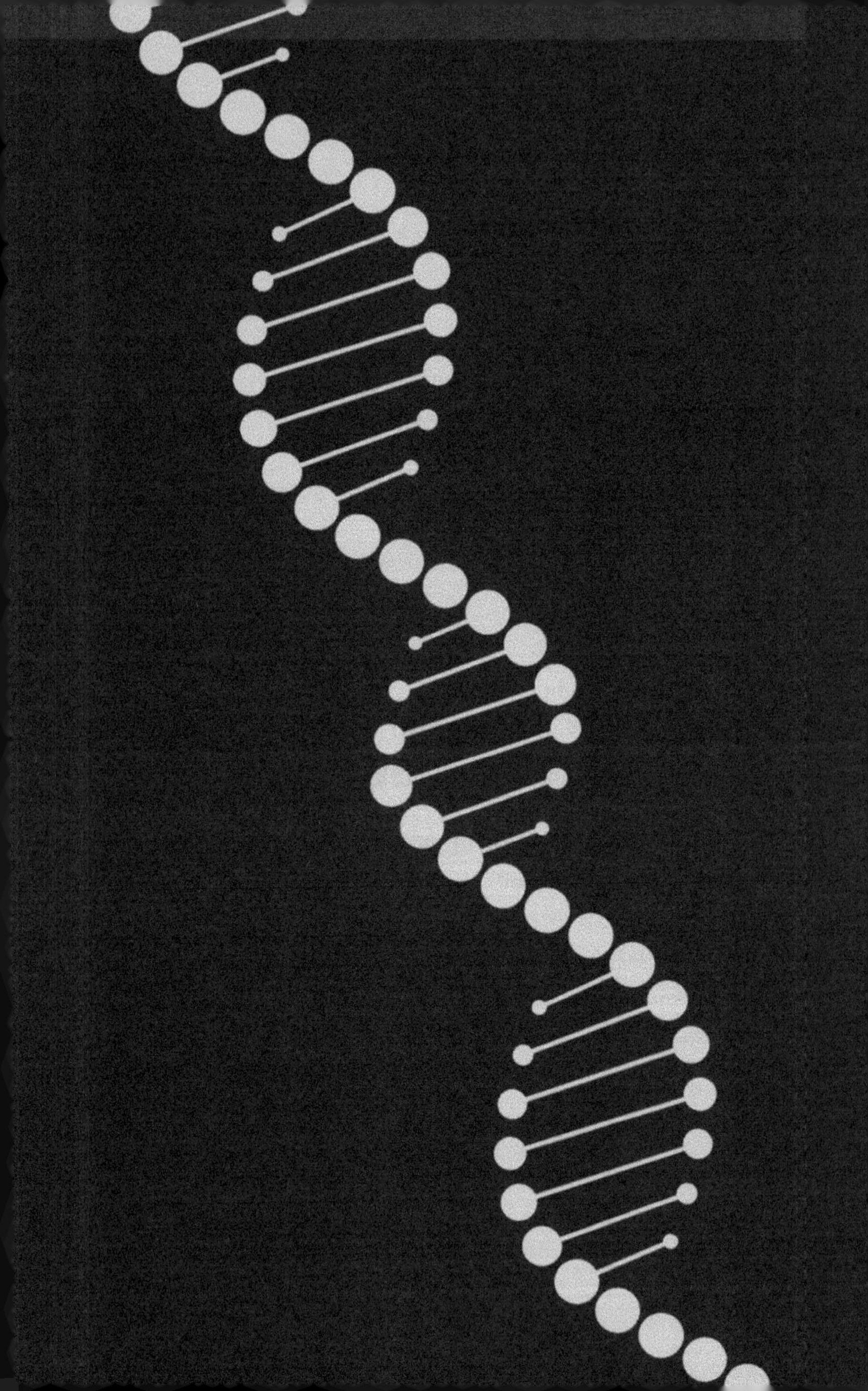

PART 1

Era of Coal

CHAPTER 1
A Girl of Singular Talent

To do any work that is worth while one needs to be passionately interested in one's subject.

—ROSALIND FRANKLIN

1933–1946, London, England

Rosalind Franklin was thirteen years old in 1933 when she discovered what could be called her greatest gift. Already pegged as an independent thinker within her family, Rosalind argued with her art teacher while doing a linocut project. Rosalind had carved a design into linoleum so that it could be covered in ink and then printed onto paper, but it wasn't up to her teacher's artistic taste. "I was told in the drawing lesson this morning, that I was too literal-minded," she wrote to her parents, grousing about her teacher's instruction. Her analytical mind was supported by her stubborn nature. No matter what her teacher tried to get her to do, Rosalind insisted that adding a flourish to her realistic image would not be correct.

So she refused.

While making her linocut prints, Rosalind realized that she was able to easily see the images backward, a requirement for printmaking. She could picture and rotate images in her mind's eye, as if they were suspended in the air in front of her. This gift, the ability to visualize a three-dimensional object, would be essential to Rosalind's monumental contributions to the world of science.

Rosalind, the second child of five, was born in 1920 into an upper-middle-class Anglo-Jewish family in Notting Hill, London. Rosalind's father, Ellis Franklin, had served in World War I (1914–1918) and afterward became a banker in London. The family was what was called "frugal rich." A friend of the family noted they were a "very, very public-spirited family." Her father volunteered as a physics teacher at London's Working Men's College, and he impressed on all his children the importance of contributing to the social welfare of others.

Unlike others in their social class, he refused to have a country house, believing that his family shouldn't have two houses when so many didn't have one. But his parents, Rosalind's grandparents, owned a vast estate in Chartridge, outside of London, where Rosalind spent many weekends with extended family. That extended family included Ellis Franklin's older sister Alice, who wore her hair short and sported men's clothing and lived with a female partner. Rosalind, growing up in conservative London society yet with family members' progressive social principles, saw both those perspectives of humanity.

In their vacation time, at Ellis Franklin's insistence, the family traveled the British Isles and parts of Europe to hike

Rosalind Franklin (*second from right*) at age twelve with her siblings Roland, David, Jenifer, and Colin.

and camp. From a young age, love for the outdoors and physical activity was a powerful motivator for Rosalind, and she was both fearless and physically strong, easily hiking steep and treacherous mountain peaks in wild, remote places. She was also observant: In a letter to her grandfather at the age of fifteen, Rosalind wrote, "We went with a guide, up on top of the glacier, 4,600 feet [1,400 m] up. It was a marvelous walk. We saw over the top of the mountains all round, and a long way down the fjord. The glacier itself was the finest thing I have ever seen." She enjoyed the travel and early on nurtured a deep love for the country of France. On a ski holiday with her brother Colin in her later teens she wrote, "It is always so much more exciting to be among people of another country."

Stubbornness and determination were family traits, and in Rosalind they were also exhibited by the physical stamina she displayed during those rigorous hikes. In one family story, after stabbing a sewing needle deep into her knee joint, Rosalind walked to a hospital on her own, to the attending doctor's astonishment. She responded by laughing.

In her family, Rosalind was known for her clear thinking—as well as what her mother, Muriel Franklin, called her "stormy" nature. She was slim and pretty, with dark hair and dark eyes that sparked when she argued a point. Rosalind fiercely debated any subject at the dinner table with her parents, three brothers, and younger sister. She questioned everything, especially her position in life. She asked her mother why God should be referred to as male, and from her earliest years, she railed against the advantages her brothers were given just because they were boys. "These storms were as a rule quickly over," her mother wrote later, "even if sometimes they were too easily provoked."

Rosalind shared her skills at debate, devotion to social welfare, and lifelong love of walking and hiking with her father. From her mother, she learned sensitivity and humor, and hands-on skills such as sewing. Her brothers challenged Rosalind to stand firm in her opinions, and her younger sister was her ally. Aunts, uncles, cousins, and grandparents surrounded her with comfort and affection and gave her a strong foundation in her Jewish heritage.

But her abiding passion from an early age was science. "Rosalind is alarmingly clever," her aunt Mamie observed in a letter to her husband when Rosalind was only six; "she spends her time doing arithmetic for pleasure and invariably gets her sums right."

Anything science-based fascinated Rosalind. While helping her mother with a home photography project, Rosalind added the photo-developing chemicals to the water and watched them dissolve. Then she submerged the exposed photo paper into the chemical bath. "It makes me feel all squidgy inside," Rosalind said, as she leaned over the tub and watched the image appear on the photo paper. This feeling would last her lifetime and, in addition to her visualization skill, forecast another talent—making images that would astonish the world.

Starting at the age of nine, Rosalind attended a series of all-girls' boarding schools and then day schools. She wrote letters to her parents complaining about those schools as well as further demonstrating her math skills. She kept tabs on her scores on tests and disputed some of her teachers' grading. "But don't tell the teachers I keep my scores, as I'm not supposed to," she begged her parents, fearing a scolding.

Rosalind's love of science and research in middle and high school spurred her to study beyond what her classes could provide. When she was seventeen, she scored one of the highest grades in chemistry exams for that year, 1938. Because that was the bar set by colleges at the time, that score gave her a place as an undergraduate at Cambridge's Newnham College, a women's campus, despite being a year younger than all but one of her classmates.

It was good she entered Newnham when she did. Only a year later, on September 1, 1939, Germany invaded Poland and started World War II (1939–1945). Two of Rosalind's brothers, older brother David and younger brother Colin, enlisted in the British Armed Forces right away, and her youngest brother Roland put off college to join the Royal Navy as the war ended. Their father volunteered to help Jewish refugees who had escaped Nazi Germany. On Rosalind's Cambridge campus, students were required to carry gas masks and dig trenches to take cover in during air raids.

Rosalind's father began to argue that this was no time for

Rosalind Franklin attended Newnham College, a place where women could reside while attending lectures at the University of Cambridge. Not until 1948 were women allowed to become full members of the University of Cambridge and granted a degree.

Rosalind to be in college and that she should do something for the benefit of their country. This was not the only time that they disagreed about Rosalind's path in life. Friends later said that her family, particularly her father, never truly understood her work in the sciences. "They would have taken more pleasure in a nice conventional daughter who did good works in charities like the rest of the family," said one close friend.

But Rosalind's will was as strong as her father's, and she responded in a letter that chemists were sure to be needed by Britain, and that she could contribute by getting her degree. "You look at science (or at least talk of it) as some sort of demoralizing invention of man, something apart from real life. . . . But science and everyday life cannot and should not be separated," she told him. "Science, for me, gives a partial explanation of life."

Studying Nobel Laureate Lawrence Bragg's work while she was at Newnham proved pivotal and united Rosalind's singular visualization gift with her early photography experience. Bragg worked in the field of X-ray crystallography, a new experimental technique that captured a beam of light when an X-ray struck a crystal. The beam of light diffracted into different directions and was then captured on film. Bragg used this technique to make a three-dimensional structural model of graphite and carbon molecules. Rosalind developed a technique using X-ray crystallography to aim the X-rays at angles that would produce the best diffraction patterns in any crystalline substance.

Meanwhile, Rosalind studied the work of American scientist Linus Pauling to learn more about nucleic acids and proteins, chemical compounds in cells that were key to understanding human DNA. Scientists knew about the existence of deoxyribonucleic acid—the material that carries genetic instructions for how living things look, grow, and function—but they didn't

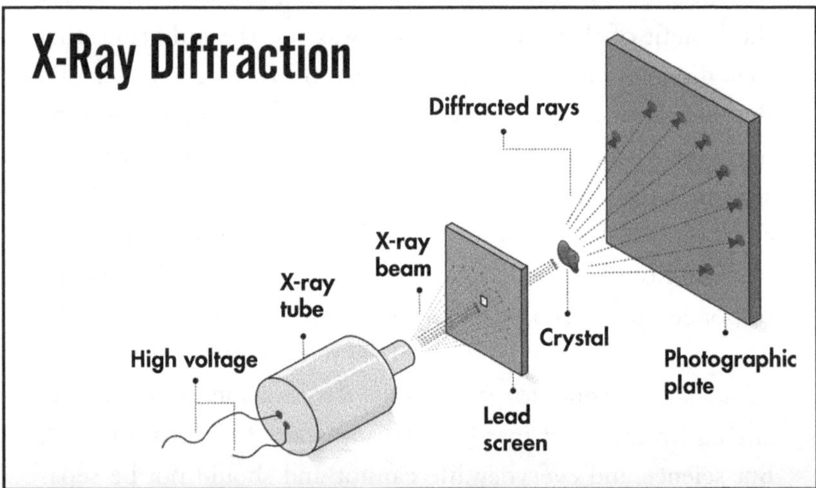

To study DNA, crystallographers would aim X-rays at crystallized DNA fibers. The rays would scatter and form patterns that were captured on diffraction plates. These patterns revealed information about DNA's structure.

know much about its structure. Using her advantage of seeing three-dimensionally in her mind's eye, Rosalind sketched in her workbook the three-dimensional molecules of graphite and carbon as Bragg had demonstrated his findings, and she related them to what she understood about DNA.

When she saw the resulting geometrical shape as a helical molecular structure, Rosalind made a leap of imagination and added a note in her workbook with the question, "Geometrical basis for inheritance?" This leap—guessing that DNA might have a math-based structure—was significant for her prescience in later figuring out the helical structure of DNA, which to that point no one fully understood.

Rosalind continued her studies at Newnham as the war raged on, throwing herself into math, chemistry, and physics, and complaining about everything from other students' ignorance—"Nobody here seems to have taken much notice of what is going on in Germany"—to being dragged to college events that would distract her from learning. She didn't care much for the social side of Cambridge. "This evening there is an awful thing called the college feast," Rosalind wrote her parents, in which the "whole college dines together in a great crush in evening dress."

Rosalind found relief from the pressure of schoolwork and war in physical activity in nature. In winter she frequented a frozen marsh not far from campus, preferring to skate there alone by moonlight. "It is surprisingly warm," she wrote, "and the ice is empty then." During the Blitz—the incessant German bombing of London in the fall of 1940—her family was forced to move to a safer home. Rosalind requested that one thing be taken with the family in that move: her Norwegian-made climbing boots, stored in a cupboard in her bedroom. She wrote, "I couldn't bear to have them bombed."

Rosalind, in her twenties, wearing her hiking boots in Norway

When she graduated from Newnham in 1941, Rosalind pursued a doctorate in chemistry. This led her to a year studying under the supervision of Ronald G. W. Norrish, professor of physical chemistry at Cambridge. She went to work with him with high hopes. But Norrish was the wrong choice to guide the strong-willed Rosalind. Norrish had a fine reputation but had slipped into personal and professional decline. Rosalind's desires to do something that would help England and the Allied Forces defeat Adolf Hitler's Nazi regime were dashed when Norrish assigned her to document his previously published results in a dull study irrelevant to the war. Worse yet, Norrish put her to work in a closetlike room, where Rosalind struggled with severe claustrophobia.

When Rosalind discovered that his results were wrong, she publicly challenged Norrish. A series of major blowups between them led Rosalind to despise Norrish. She confronted him, and afterward, she wrote to a friend that "he became most offensive and we had a first-class row—in fact, several." He wouldn't accept being wrong, especially from a young female student. She decided she had to leave his lab because he was "stupid, bigoted, deceitful, ill-mannered and tyrannical." Rosalind did not then, nor after, suffer fools. Instead of a mentor, Norrish was the first of many scientists who disappointed her by producing shoddy work. And her experience with Norrish cemented Rosalind's belief in the principle of scientific fact over guessing.

1942, BCURA near London

In 1942, three years into the war and when she was twenty-two, Rosalind rented a room in a hostel owned by Adrienne Weill. Weill was a Cambridge professor and French-born scientist whom Rosalind had met while she was still an undergrad. Weill balanced her career with raising her young daughter and became

Rosalind's role model—and someone with whom she could practice her French. The two would become lifelong friends.

With Weill's guidance, Rosalind left Norrish's lab and went to work at the British Coal Utilisation Research Association (BCURA) lab to study the structure of coal. At BCURA, Rosalind's assignment, which could lead her to a PhD, was to examine the different types of coal and understand coal's permeability, or how water and gas flowed through the pores or channels within coal cells. Rosalind did not use a normal light-reflecting microscope for these analyses. Instead, she used an electron microscope for X-ray crystallography, with the technology and techniques she'd learned from Bragg.

In her analyses of coal, she could imagine the molecular structures she saw through the lens as if they floated in space before her, as she had when she made her linocut years earlier. This ability led her to publish groundbreaking results, as she developed her own techniques of heating and cooling the carbon molecules to study when and how holes or openings within the cells formed.

As a BCURA assistant research officer who was not certified in using machine tools, Rosalind wasn't authorized to use the workshop equipment for her analyses as she experimented with trying to pass helium through the pores in coal. But the determined Rosalind didn't let signs in the shop put her off. She turned them over and used the equipment to get her work done.

Within a few years at BCURA, Rosalind's microscopic coal analyses were known throughout the field. Her publications earned her an international reputation in helping with the war effort, because her research on carbon structure influenced the types of carbon filters used in gas masks—which would save many lives from the effects of the chemical warfare waged during World War II. And her work earned her a doctorate degree,

Rosalind at the Cabane des Evettes in the French Alps

which she finished at the age of twenty-four just as the war was ending in 1945.

After the war, Rosalind wrote to Weill as she sought her next steps: "If ever you hear of anybody anxious for the services of a physical chemist who knows very little about physical chemistry but a lot about the holes in coal, please let me know." Weill invited renowned French crystallographer Jacques Mering to Rosalind's 1946 lecture on her coal analysis resultsat the Royal

Institution of Great Britain. Mering, impressed with Rosalind's work, offered her a position at his lab in Paris, France, and she accepted. Mering would become an important figure in the rest of Rosalind's life.

That summer Rosalind packed her beloved hiking boots and took off with her school friend Jean Kerslake for a hiking adventure in the French Alps. They traversed the high mountains in precarious conditions and stayed in spartan hostels, sharing wine and cigarettes with fellow travelers. "I am quite sure I could wander happily in France for ever," she wrote home. "I love the people, the country, and the food."

She would start her position with Jacques Mering and his team early in 1947, two years after the war ended. She was ready to break away from her family, ready to take her visualization gift and analytic work to a new level in a new place—and Rosalind was more than ready to be exposed to a wider world, especially when that exposure led her to Paris.

CHAPTER 2

In the City of Lights

When she arrived in Paris in February 1947, Rosalind quickly became, in D.D. Lawrence's word, "unEnglished".

—BRENDA MADDOX

1947–1951, Laboratoire Central des Services Chimiques de l'État in Paris, France

In late winter 1947, with a new bobbed haircut, twenty-six-year-old Rosalind walked along the Seine River on her way to the French State Laboratory for the Study of Chemistry, the Laboratoire Central des Services Chimiques de l'État, known by those who worked there as the "Labo." Compared with the pea soup fog at home, the air was clear and clean, and Paris itself, unlike Blitz-bombed London, was remarkably whole.

Rosalind had joined the Labo in February of that year. Paris was the place she'd dreamed of returning to, saying after a six-week trip at the age of eighteen, "I shall be very sorry to leave." From fabulous food to stylish clothing to stimulating work to a growing network of close friends, Rosalind adapted quickly to her new life. Rosalind especially loved this walk along the river, telling her brother Colin that it was "a fresh thrill every day." She preferred walking or cycling to taking the Metro anyway, owing to her claustrophobia.

She was always glad to be out of her tiny, frigid apartment, and especially happy to head to work in the lab, which had windows with views of the Seine. Friends at home had joked that she would find true love in the City of Lights. As far as Rosalind was concerned, she found something better. She was able to work with a group of like-minded scientists whom she respected and who treated her with respect. "Though my circle is naturally smaller than in London," Rosalind wrote to her parents, ". . . I find infinite kindness and goodwill among the people I work with."

She was paid—not a lot, but enough for her living expenses—and given the freedom to work further on the microstructure of coal using X-ray crystallography, expanding what she'd already discovered about carbons and graphites. Her ingenuity and quick mind impressed her new French colleagues. She was meticulous and loved tinkering with the equipment, making repairs to the microscopes using supplies brought from England by Colin. Rosalind's skill at tinkering was beneficial because the most elementary lab items, such as silicon wax, were lacking. But owing to her skills and her brother's aid, Rosalind was able to keep making measurements.

The postwar shortages affected Rosalind personally as well. She was deeply sensitive to the worsened wealth gap, as she had been from her early years under her family's influence. She told her parents that the standard ration was intolerably low, and that she didn't know how people managed. While the war had spared Paris's buildings, it had created serious food and supply shortages in France as well as everywhere else in Europe. Bread was rationed, eggs were expensive, and even milk was at times unobtainable.

But unlike those around her, because of the help she received from her family and her position as a foreign employee, Rosalind had a little money to spend on luxuries. One of those luxuries was an indulgence in the latest Paris fashion. From the moment she arrived in the city, she began changing her style of dress from school-girl English to beautiful French clothes, especially the Dior New Look silhouette. Having learned how to sew from her mother, she often made her own clothes in those fashions. Her friends observed that she was always beautifully dressed, and her figure—she was tiny and small-waisted—was perfectly suited for the long full skirts with cinched and belted waists popular in postwar France.

In addition to knowing how to sew, she shared her mother's teasing wit and friendly exuberance, which brought friends naturally to her side. She was close to the family she left behind in London but was thrilled to be independent after the stifling war years and her frustrating experience with Norrish. She told Colin, "Freedom is the thing I appreciate most in this new life. It is what I came for and I have found it."

Rosalind took long lunches each day with her colleagues in a small restaurant, Chez Solange, near the lab. After work, she and her friends gathered at a sidewalk café, sipping coffee and arguing about politics or scientific principles. She enjoyed Parisian culture, attending the theater and movies, visiting the museums, going dancing at night, and taking in some of the more interesting cultural events: "I went last night to an American roller-skating show which drew a crowd of 30,000."

Rosalind lived near the Church of Saint-Sulpice and the Palais du Luxembourg, easily within walking distance to work.

Her apartment was a small room without heat, hot water, or a place to bathe. Part of the room's decor was a plaster cast of a dead man's face—the death mask of the dour landlady's husband. Rosalind put up with the room with good cheer, saying to Colin, "It was so gloomy as to be funny." She was only allowed to use the kitchen once her landlady had eaten supper, but the maid taught Rosalind the basics of French cooking in those after-hours.

A visiting cousin expressed shock at her living conditions and especially the absence of a bath. Rosalind tried to make him feel better "by reminding him that I could have a bath in May." She also put up with a lack of wood to keep her room warm, saying, "I would willingly go more primitive if it were necessary to preserve my freedom." Rosalind made it clear to all her family that her freedom in Paris, her lively scientific relationships, and her research were "far more important than a large meat ration or more frequent baths."

She took advantage of her free time to travel, and especially to take in her second love: walking and hiking. In the Grande Casse, a mountain summit in France, Rosalind and her guide made the ascent at 3:30 a.m. She fearlessly followed the guide's lantern along ice ridges to see the sunrise from the peak. Articulate as always when describing the scenery, she told Colin that it was a "wonderful moment when the sun flashes onto the mountain tops and rapidly covers the whole earth with the dazzling early morning pink."

Rosalind wrote to her parents, "I would write for weeks about the flowers on the mountains . . . things like pale mauve crocuses, French marigolds, deep purple hairbells, Woolworths cactuses, all sorts of rock plants, thistles the size of cabbages." She also enjoyed the more entertaining aspects of travel, adding, "Saturday I spent mainly visiting Strasbourg labs and tasting superb Alsace wines, and Sunday I spent on the back of a motorcycle, and again tasting wines."

Rosalind took a bicycle tour through Tuscany, Italy, with Vittorio Luzzati, another X-ray crystallographer at her lab, and his wife Denise. Rosalind shared a similar temperament with Luzzati, and they shared adjoining rooms in the Labo. They both held strong opinions about politics and science, and both were keenly intelligent. She and Luzzati were famous for their heated yet friendly arguments, in sharp contrast with the rows she'd had with Norrish. Their friendship would last throughout her life.

Rosalind pauses during a bike ride in Tuscany.

Her work with Mering, Luzzati, and the other lab scientists was collaborative and fruitful. Mering was an expert in crystallography, and she was a brilliant pupil. The science aspect of Rosalind's life was perfect.

But did Rosalind find love in Paris, as her friends believed she would?

Jacques Mering was a Russian-born Jew, handsome, and charismatic—and married. The normally reserved Rosalind sparkled in his presence, chatting with him in fluent French. She loved being able to share her scientific insights with a charming, intelligent mentor. In England, friends said she went through "a scruffy period and did not really pay much attention to clothes until she went to Paris." But in France, Rosalind bloomed, and her friends believed it was because she was in love with Mering.

Rosalind was emotionally young for her age. Her parents had sheltered her from making social connections with boys. Before moving to Paris, she had never dated and was ignorant of romance. When she met Mering, she might have had a schoolgirl crush on the older man. But Mering was a father with at least one mistress with whom he also had a child. Denise Luzzati said, "With Rosalind it might not have been much of an affair—Rosalind was truly innocent—but . . . it was something with a good deal of emotion attached to it."

Brenda Maddox, Rosalind's biographer, noted, "Adrienne Weill was well aware of Rosalind's feelings for Mering, which she saw as deep, genuine, and somewhat tragic."

Rosalind only admitted much later to her friend Anne Sayre that she had been in love with Mering. Mering also admitted later that he had loved her and he "felt sure she was in love with him." But he added that Rosalind "was naïve and inexperienced and could not lightly enter into" whatever it was he had in mind. "She had very high and rather narrow standards of the proper behavior—scientifically and personally," Mering said, "and could grow 'formidable' when these were transgressed."

Others were also aware of Rosalind's high standards. Close friend Margaret North said, "Rosalind could be quite scathing with people who made mistakes."

Biochemist Bocha Altmann said, "Rosalind couldn't have married anyone who did not, above all, command her deepest respect: this need to think of one's husband not only as 'very good but absolutely superior.'"

Vittorio Luzzati said, "There was in Rosalind a psychological knot that I was never able to analyze; it might have had to do with an experience during the war, with her education, or something else. She was very strong and crushing, very demanding of herself and others, enduring not always to be liked."

Mering believed that Rosalind's feelings for him "made it impossible for her to form other attachments." He said a man named Pierre Hirsch was "much in love with Rosalind and wanted to marry her, but she would have no part of this." Mering also spoke about a French mathematician "who courted Rosalind assiduously, and was madly in love with her, but Rosalind couldn't see this either."

Complicating the possibility of a love life was Rosalind's growing belief that a woman couldn't be both a professional and a mother, despite the example set by Adrienne Weill. Denise Luzzati said that Rosalind was amazed and shocked that Denise continued to work after becoming a mother. "She didn't condemn me," Denise said, "but I could see that she thought it was strange, or unwise—she was worried about Anne [Denise's daughter]. Rosalind believed that a woman could marry or have a career but that the two—especially if the woman had children—were incompatible." She added, "Rosalind deliberately chose one alternative rather than the other as if these alternatives were true ones."

While Paris was a transformative place in many ways for Rosalind, it didn't provide her with a family of her own.

By 1949, Rosalind's parents put increasing pressure on her to return to London. Rosalind was torn. She recognized that her roots, her family, and greater scientific opportunity waited for her in England. But Rosalind had matured as both a woman and a scientist in those three years. The work she had done at Mering's lab and the guidance she received from him allowed her to reach a new level of competence in X-ray diffraction and crystallography, and she was by this time a world expert in the structure of carbon. Should she stay in France? Or return to England?

She wrote to Colin of her "preference for Paris, the French way of life, the mass of French people and (not a negligible factor) the Parisian climate." In Paris, she had been free to do the thing she loved best: useful science. But she'd reached a natural plateau in her career, and perhaps in her personal life. A clear-headed consideration of her future finally forced Rosalind's hand. She wrote to Charles Coulson of King's College, London, about the possibility of a fellowship.

Coulson wanted her to come to King's to work on something new: the biological applications of X-ray crystallography.

During her interview, he introduced her to John T. Randall, the director of the King's College biophysics lab. Randall offered her a job using her skills to study proteins. But before her departure from Paris, Randall changed her assignment from examining the structures of proteins to examining the crystalline structure of DNA. This change in Rosalind's job description came at the suggestion of the lab's assistant director and head of the biophysics unit, Maurice Wilkins, and would have monumental consequences for all involved, especially when Wilkins later claimed he never made it.

"After very careful consideration and discussion with the senior people concerned," Randall wrote to Rosalind, "it now seems a good deal more important for you to investigate the structure of certain biological fibers . . . both by high and low angle diffractions rather than to continue with the original project of work on solutions as the major one. Dr. Stokes . . . really wishes to concern himself almost entirely with theoretical problems in the future. . . . This means that as far as the experimental X-ray effort is concerned there will be at the moment only yourself and Raymond Gosling."

Rosalind was hesitant, replying to Randall that "I am, of course, most ignorant about all things biological." But she was smart enough to recognize the possibilities of working in an emerging, even groundbreaking scientific field. So she said yes.

In the winter of 1951, Rosalind felt the sharp pain of leaving France. Regardless of the pull of family and the opportunities provided by this new position at King's, her departure from Paris would leave a vast hole in her heart, and she was already regretting her decision. It was a hole she could fill only by dedication to her study of DNA, but she wondered whether it would be filled with as much joy as she'd experienced in France.

Studying DNA

Uncovering a literal blueprint for how a life is structured and how a life functions seemed out of reach for much of scientific history. Like a good mystery, each discovery came to scientists in pieces. Before Rosalind studied genes and DNA in the mid-1900s, there was . . .

A Monk, His Pea Plants, and Invisible Factors

In 1866 a monk named Gregor Mendel ran an experiment on pea plants. He considered seven characteristics: the plant's height, pod shape, pod color, seed shape, seed color, flower position, and flower color. He found that if a yellow pea seed and a green pea seed were bred together, it would always result in a yellow plant. But in the next generation of plants, the green peas reappeared at a ratio of 1:3. The monk wrote a paper about the way in which traits are passed from one generation to the next and how the traits sometimes skip generations. Mendel came up with the concept of dominant and recessive traits. For peas, a yellow color is dominant, while green is recessive. Mendel called these "invisible factors." We refer to Mendel's invisible factors as genes.

In the early 1900s Danish scientist Wilhelm Johannsen applied this to human traits. For example, every human cell contains two genes that represent eye color. Brown eyes are dominant, and blue eyes are recessive. So, if a person inherits a gene for brown eyes from each parent, they will have brown eyes. If they inherit a gene for blue eyes from each parent, they will have blue eyes. But if they inherit one gene for brown eyes and one gene for blue, they will have brown eyes because that is the dominant trait.

A Chemist and Used Surgical Bandages

In 1869 Swiss chemist Friedrich Miescher set out to study the content of white blood cells called leukocytes. White blood cells

One of the first biochemistry labs in the world, Miescher's lab was at one point located in a kitchen in a castle in Tübigen, Germany.

fight infections, and they are abundant in wounds. So, Miescher collected discarded surgical bandages. In a primitive lab, he washed the bandages with different solutions until he separated the leukocytes from the rest of the blood cells.

Miescher isolated a molecule rich in phosphate from the cell's nucleus and called it nuclein. Miescher thought the nuclein was an important clue to how cells function. He and other scientists believed the molecule might hold the traits passed from parents to children. Indeed, the slimy substance (puss from the bandages he examined) contained the molecule that carried genetic information. Nuclein turned out to be the molecule of heredity itself. We refer to this molecule as DNA. The "N" in DNA refers to Miescher's nuclein, and it's now called nucleic acid.

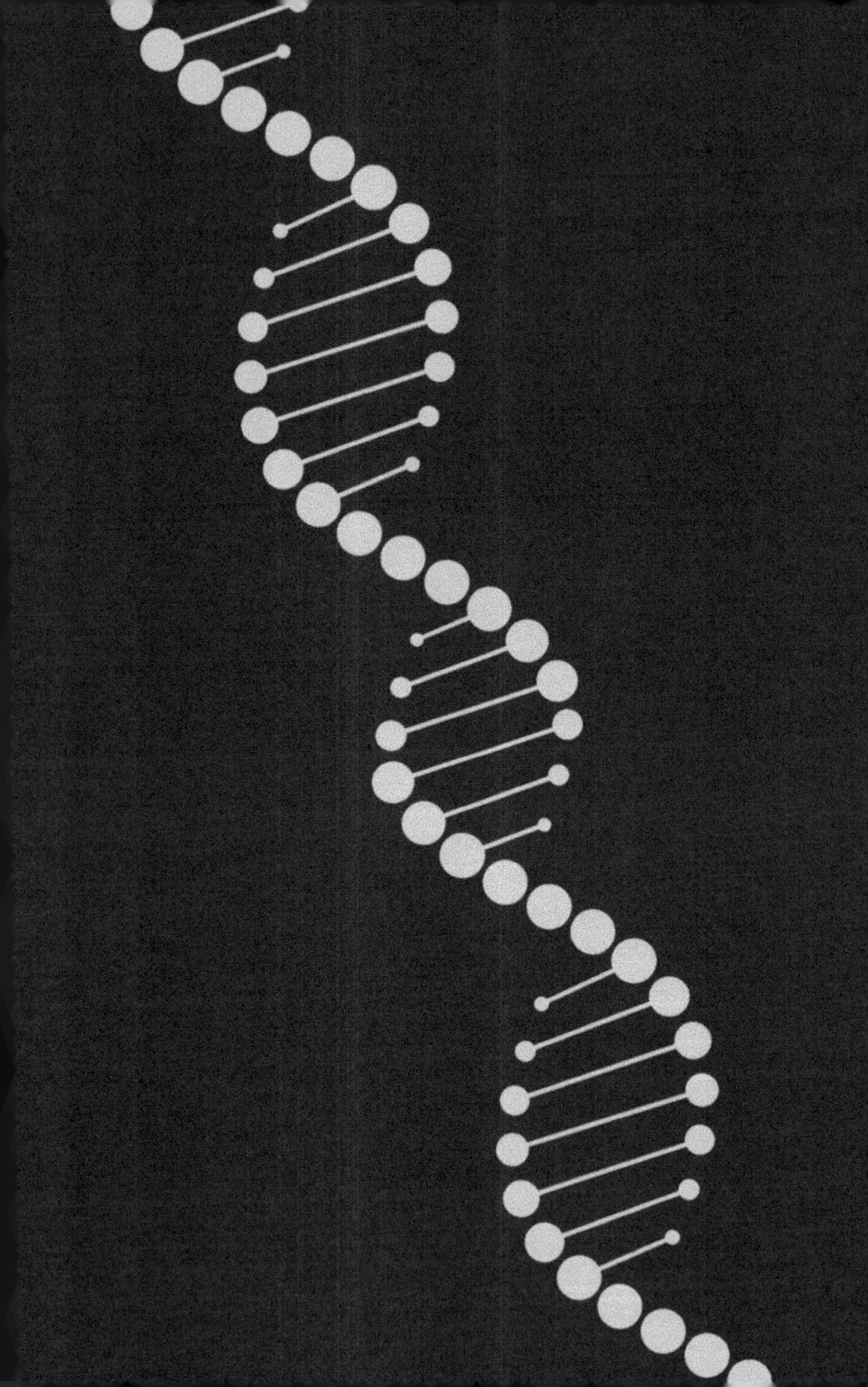

PART 2

Era of the Double Helix

CHAPTER 3

Moving Back to London

I knew she had studied coal for 4 years in a leading X-ray lab in Paris but I did not know until later that she had been in charge of all her research, and had become the world's expert on the structure of coal and related substances.

—MAURICE WILKINS

January 1951, King's College Biophysics Lab in London, England

A massive crater stood between Rosalind and her new assignment. At King's College, she trekked around the hole in the ground that had scarred the research university's quad—27 feet (8.2 m) deep by 58 feet (17.7 m) long—courtesy of a bomb dropped ten years earlier during the war. Britain had suffered a much deeper level of destruction than Rosalind's beloved Paris.

The bombed-out places in London were sad reminders of the many things that had vanished from her daily life, including her walk to work past the Seine and Notre Dame. Back in London, she was served fake cream on top of her fruit at a local café, and she longed for Parisian sidewalk cafés and their savory toppings. The war had ended six years earlier, but Britain was still under food rations. "What is it that makes my home country seem so awful after returning from living in a foreign country that I've come to love?" Rosalind complained to her friend Anne Sayre. "I was so much happier in France, and London now seems dreary by comparison."

King's College administrators planned to build new labs for the Biophysics Department in the place where the bomb had demolished the quad. But meanwhile, Rosalind's lab and office were in a windowless basement beneath the parking garage. The furniture arrangement in her office meant that her back would be to the door. Hoping for another friendly lab environment, Rosalind hung a mirror on the wall facing her desk to alert herself to visitors. This way, when a coworker popped in, she could wave them over to her desk to chat. And the mirror made the space feel a little bigger, helping to stave off her claustrophobia.

Rosalind hoped to re-create the collaborative working environment she had in Paris. The constant flow of research conversation, including during café lunches, had been so important to her work there. But on arriving at King's and while being shown her new lab, she learned that the scientists' dining room, known as the Senior Common Room, was exclusively available to male staff and not open to women. When the senior male scientists gathered in that room, Rosalind and the other women—grad students, secretaries, and senior researchers alike—were relegated to a secondary assistants' dining room or had to eat at a local restaurant. The men didn't like having to observe proprieties that they felt necessary if women were present. And including women after centuries of exclusion was a step too far. Rosalind learned that the men didn't talk shop in that room anyway, and they worried that the women would bring work into their clubby space.

Rosalind had been torn about taking the position at King's and told some friends that she thought about backing out, saying, "I still spend at least half my time wondering—very seriously—whether to chuck up the whole thing and stay here [in Paris]." But she was close with her family, and now she was home again. And so, despite the less-than-ideal work conditions, Rosalind was determined to make the work meaningful, and she knew that she'd been hired in a cutting-edge field.

Rosalind would be working with two colleagues: Raymond Gosling and Alec Stokes. Stokes was King's distinguished mathematician, and Gosling was a star PhD student with experience in X-ray diffraction. The three scientists would be blending biology and physics into the new science of biophysics to understand DNA's structure through crystallography. Randall made it clear right away that Stokes and Gosling would be working under Rosalind's guidance. Recalling Randall's instruction, Gosling said later, "I was formally handed over . . . to Rosalind who would now be my day-to-day supervisor." Stokes would review the mathematical calculations that Rosalind and Gosling required, and Gosling would do the experimental work at Rosalind's side.

The missing member of the biophysics unit, Maurice Wilkins, had been Gosling's supervisor. But Wilkins was away on a vacation with a friend's nanny when Rosalind arrived at King's. Although Rosalind's reassignment to work on DNA was originally Wilkins's suggestion, Wilkins had assumed she would be his subordinate. His absence at her arrival, these

Raymond Gosling in 1960

introductions, the reassignment of Gosling, and Wilkins's ignorance of Randall's actions, would lead to haunting negative consequences for all involved.

Gosling, an agreeable and hardworking young man, knew of Rosalind's reputation and her work on carbon, and was delighted with this turn of events. He could see right away that Rosalind's approach was very different compared with Wilkins's. If Gosling asked questions of Wilkins, he made it clear that he didn't want to be interrupted, taking Gosling's questions as challenges rather than as an exchange of ideas. Gosling was sure Rosalind would elevate his research and thesis to the next level. And for her part, Rosalind vowed not to echo the dreadful experience she had working with Norrish on her doctorate. As Gosling's new superior, she would provide an open door and open mind, a partnership in which Gosling brought her ideas, and she listened.

Rosalind, for her part, was relieved to meet Gosling and Stokes. Never mind the basement office and the exclusive dining room, she was ready to build a great team. She and Gosling formed a lifelong friendship that led to breakthroughs despite (or maybe because of) their isolation from the other male scientists at King's. This was her chance to create a lab experience like she'd had in Paris where colleagues continued their discussions well past working hours and bonded over the science—an atmosphere where mutual respect was paramount.

She paid close attention as Gosling filled her in on the progress, or lack of progress, the King's lab had made thus far on DNA analysis. Gosling and Wilkins had had trouble getting useful X-ray crystallography images of the lab's two primary DNA samples—from a ram and a calf. Gosling later said, "It was my job of taking the specimens and getting them to lie down side-by-side and flat. Well, you can imagine how tricky that was. And I had about six different ways of trying to do that. The idea was I'd get a lot of them flat and then I'd stand the flat sheet or I would shine the X-rays through and I'd get the X-ray diffraction pattern of the stuff inside. But I was getting nowhere."

After using the ram sample, Gosling then worked with a DNA sample from a calf thymus—an organ that is part of the immune system—that was produced by biochemist Rudolf Signer. Signer had brought samples of calf thymus DNA to a conference lecture at the University of Bern in early 1950. Wilkins had attended the conference and acquired a few of what became known as the Signer DNA set and transported them back to King's lab.

Signer had recognized that as a long chain molecule, DNA could be easily fragmented. Signer produced samples better suited to X-ray crystallography because they were more viscous than anything else available at the time. The Signer samples' purity, thickness, and weight were superior to Gosling's ram specimen and made less blurry images.

Each of the small glass bottles of Signer DNA were filled about a third of the way with what looked like balls of cotton pulled from a fraying sweater. These DNA samples were prepared in a dry form, and Gosling and Wilkins had tried creating a hydrated sample. The trick was to hydrate DNA fibers to mimic the conditions of DNA in living organisms. "I had

Barger's Method

The ram sample had been prepared with a technique invented by chemist George Barger in 1904. But Barger's experimental method had been used to weigh material thinner than DNA. The viscosity of DNA, a gelatinous material, wasn't well suited to the Barger process, which worked fine for less tacky material. Gosling told Rosalind that he wound up taking confusing images of overlapping patterns. The photographs were blurry at best.

a paper clip," Gosling said, "and I wound the fibers round the paper clip and then I glued them with quick setting cement that I bought from Woolworth's down the road in Strand and pulled the clip apart to tension them. Then I took that over to the chemistry department where we had an old X-ray diffraction tube and the rest, as they say, is history."

The image Gosling produced from this technique was better than his earlier images. Gosling told Rosalind that he felt it was his "Eureka" moment because it proved that DNA fibers could be crystallized. But it still wasn't perfect.

Rosalind listened to Gosling's report with interest. These were challenges she knew she could solve. Her first task was to reengineer some of the lab's equipment to minimize the scatter of the air in the camera by sending a steady stream of hydrogen into the chamber. That hydrogen stream would keep the chamber in a constant state of humidity, which was vital for observing the waxy and dry DNA fibers. Rosalind knew that the lab's existing equipment was not capable of imaging these small samples with the right measure of hydrogen, so within a few hours in her new job she got straight to business.

She sat on the floor of the lab underneath the equipment and took apart the X-ray crystallography system and reconfigured it. Where new parts were required, she designed them and sent them to be made by the team in the Physics Department's workshop. She also incorporated a prototype X-ray tube developed by Werner Ehrenberg that had been given to Wilkins. An X-ray tube is a device that generates X-rays by accelerating electrons and directing them to strike a metal target. This was another of her superpowers, born out of her passion for tinkering: not only could she analyze the results of X-ray crystallography, but she also redesigned and rebuilt the equipment that she needed to analyze the specimens.

When Maurice Wilkins returned from vacation several weeks after Rosalind's arrival, he was shocked to find Rosalind and Gosling using his equipment and his Signer DNA samples. Rosalind and Gosling had developed a strong working relationship in a very short time. And they'd made progress in an experiment that Wilkins had all but abandoned due to his repeated failures.

For several years, Wilkins and a colleague, Bill Seeds, had tried to patent and build an original design for a simple reflecting microscope. But by the time they'd obtained the patent, their design was already out of date. Wilkins's ongoing attempts to contract with a microscope manufacturer for an expensive piece of equipment that was no longer cutting edge were an embarrassing failure.

What must have really rankled Wilkins, who considered

himself an expert in microscopy, was Rosalind's reconfiguration of his lab's equipment. In the few weeks while Wilkins was away, Rosalind had assumed command of the entire DNA program, made off with Wilkins's doctoral student, and redesigned the King's X-ray diffraction system to better analyze the Signer DNA samples that Wilkins had brought back from Bern.

Rosalind and Wilkins took an instant dislike to each other. Though they were close in age, they were opposites in personality. Rosalind was blunt and opinionated, looking straight into the eyes of whomever she was talking to—lessons learned from growing up with her three obstinate brothers and debate-loving father. Wilkins struggled with lifelong depression and feelings of inadequacy. He avoided conflict and direct eye contact, physically turning away from Rosalind while speaking.

When Hydrogen Was Called Inflammable Air

In 1766 Henry Cavendish was the first to recognize hydrogen gas as a discrete substance. It was not yet named "hydrogen." Instead, he called it "inflammable air." One of the richest men in London, he was reclusive and spent much of his time in his private lab. Cavendish Lab at Cambridge University, which appears later in this book, was named after him.

Antoine Lavoisier, in 1783, gave the discrete substance its official elemental name, hydrogen. In Greek, *hydro* means "water" and *gen* means "race, birth, born, or creator."

Even people who knew Wilkins and considered themselves his friends described him as neurotic. Tall, thin, with a tendency to mumble, he disliked confrontation, and had old-fashioned and misogynistic views about women, in both marriage (his own had failed miserably) and the workplace.

Rosalind was his equal or better in intelligence and had no trouble making her abilities clear, which unnerved Wilkins. Her childhood habit of arguing, honed by her Paris years of scholarly argument with friends such as Vittorio Luzzati, was the worst thing she could inflict on Wilkins. From his awkward behavior toward her to his treatment of Gosling to what she considered his scientific failures, she couldn't stand him. She didn't suffer fools, and she pegged Wilkins for a fool.

As Wilkins resumed his efforts in the lab, Rosalind watched him with growing impatience and finally intervened. Rosalind told him that "the sample's water bath should be infused with a salt solution," speaking to him as if he was an undergrad. He ignored Rosalind's advice, taking it as an insult.

Gosling said, "Rosalind would say, 'You're wrong, . . . And this is why you are wrong: one, two, three, four, five, six, seven—and if you can't see it, you're a stupid fool.' And she'd say so, bing!"

When Rosalind turned out to be correct, Wilkins fumed, complaining in the pub to his male colleagues. This irritating young woman embarrassed him in his own lab. Wilkins accused her of being pushy and superior and passed off her correct experimental approach as being accidental. Wilkins left Rosalind notes dictating what he wanted her to do. But she ignored them. He then complained to Randall and insisted that Rosalind be told she was Wilkins's assistant. Randall did nothing. Of the situation, James Watson, a young American molecular biologist and Wilkins's colleague, said that "she [Rosalind] had been given DNA for her own problem and would not think of herself as Maurice's assistant."

Wilkins mumbled something in return to Rosalind's critiques and continued to complain behind her back. If it crossed Wilkins's mind that he might be revealed as a poor team player, he didn't care. Watson grumbled, "The best home for a feminist is in another person's lab."

Two decades later, Randall said, "at no time was Rosalind Wilkins 'assistant' . . . she was an independent worker and was in no way subject to Wilkins." Wilkins saw Randall's redesigned hierarchy and Rosalind's usurpation as a betrayal, and the upset lit an ember that continued to smolder.

To make matters worse, Wilkins's collaborator Bill Seeds reinforced the misogyny of the lab, and that only resulted in more animosity. When Seeds suggested changes to Rosalind's camera stand, she said (and she was correct), "You're completely wrong." Seeds gave Rosalind the diminutive nickname "Rosy," even going so far as to hang up the sign "Rosy's Parlour" over her equipment, a play on the idea of a magician conjuring tricks and implying that she was making magic instead of science. She didn't find this funny, hating the nickname because it implied that she was flighty and incapable.

They are all "little schoolboys," she told friends in disgust.

Gosling sensed the toxic atmosphere at King's and said, "It's known as Randall's circus but to the people in it, it was more of a club than a lab." And a men's club for certain.

In a shaky attempt to reinsert himself into the research, Wilkins claimed to Randall that while on his holiday, he'd decided to abandon his microscope research and go back to DNA analysis. He also insisted that he'd had no idea Rosalind had been hired, when it had been his suggestion. Despite Rosalind's scientific expertise, Wilkins became determined to take center stage, and—ignoring all scientific propriety—he decided that an upcoming conference might give him his chance to reestablish himself as the King's' DNA project leader.

Rosalind forged ahead with her work. She knew she was on the cusp of exciting scientific discoveries at King's. But she did not have that Paris feeling. And regardless of her success, the personal atmosphere in the King's lab would not improve.

CHAPTER 4

Go Back to Your Microscopes

To let sexist aspects of life get in the way of attaining proper work relations in the workplace is, of course, a sexist lapse, though in this case, I think not in itself a very serious one, though its consequences were serious.

—MAURICE WILKINS

May–July 1951, King's College Biophysics Lab in London and Cambridge University in Cambridge, England

Besides her work at King's, Rosalind also had a social circle in London. In fact, she had three different social sets: work, family, and friends, and she was a different person with each. When she was in the lab, Rosalind was reserved and businesslike with her male colleagues.

When she was with her family, Rosalind put up with her father's conservatism and her mother's bemoaning the "Communist" influence the French had on Rosalind.

"Her family doesn't really understand her very well," said one of the graduate students at King's. "But while she disagrees with them about a lot if things, she's always careful to spend more time doing things for them than I've ever done for my family."

And as for her social life, Gosling said, "I saw her occasionally when she was going to the opera. And that was a shiny Rosalind with eyes that sparkled. Certainly, looked quite lovely."

Rosalind lived by herself in a flat, and there she found the happiest aspect of her new London life. She loved having guests over and laughed and debated good-naturedly with friends and colleagues. Having her own kitchen at last, she also loved to entertain. She used what she'd learned about French cooking while in Paris and became renowned as an excellent cook, specializing in rabbit, pigeon, and roast beef—accented with lots of garlic, butter, and olive oil. One friend called Rosalind an elegant hostess, "[serving] marvelous French food, and everything so gracefully done."

Her dinner parties, attended by members of her family as well as Raymond Gosling and a small group of colleagues from the King's lab (but never attended by Maurice Wilkins), were famous for great conversation and for the gifts she put at each guest's place setting. Rosalind put "a lot of time in doing little things that perhaps aren't so little to make things nice for people," said one friend.

Her mother bragged that Rosalind always dressed in up-to-date styles, a holdover from her Paris years. She continued to sew and make her own clothes. Her work uniform was a crisp white shirt and dark skirt topped off by a white lab coat, but in off-hours she wore floral cotton dresses that accented her small waist.

Rosalind did have some romantic attachments in London. At one point, she dated the first violinist of the London Philharmonic. But she continued to question whether a woman could be both a professional and have a family. She frequently mentioned to friends that if she was to be a scientist, she couldn't become a mother, as it wouldn't be fair to the children. This sentiment was one of many that kept Rosalind focused on her work.

In just those first months back in London, Rosalind's assignment at King's was picking up steam. The success she was having in the lab often gave her that same breathless feeling as the peaks she'd ascended in the Alps. She'd rebuilt the X-ray crystallography machine to include the prototype Ehrenberg X-ray tube, her fine focus camera, and the perfect amount of hydrogen. She'd adapted all aspects of the King's lab to suit her skills, and she and Gosling were taking the first quality images of the Signer DNA. These images were superior to the "Eureka" photograph Gosling had taken using the dime-store cement to keep fibers flat. Rosalind and Gosling were on the right track.

Their excitement was not shared by Wilkins. Chafing against his loss of stature in the King's lab, Wilkins was crafting something else altogether. A conference on large molecules held in Naples, Italy, on May 22 was his opportunity to take back the spotlight. Randall had been scheduled to attend the conference but couldn't, and neither could Rosalind. Randall asked Wilkins, as his deputy director, to go in his place. Randall had planned to give a general update on the King's DNA work, but he ordered Wilkins to present a paper on proteins. Randall

Maurice Wilkins

didn't want Wilkins discussing the DNA research for two reasons: Randall had given Rosalind the reins, and he and every biophysicist knew that leaking even small bits of information on early DNA results might prompt someone else to solve the mystery of DNA's structure first.

Rosalind was happy when Wilkins left for Naples. She and Gosling could make strides without Wilkins skulking in the background mumbling complaints.

The Naples conference keynote speaker was William Astbury from the University of Leeds. Astbury, like Rosalind, specialized in X-ray crystallography and had dabbled in imaging DNA. Thirteen years earlier, Astbury's PhD student Florence Bell had produced the first image suggesting that DNA structure was regular and ordered. Bell's image was blurry, and Astbury described the structure as looking like a "pile of pennies."

Despite its indistinct shape, Astbury, proud of Bell's work and hoping to spur conversation about the subject, showed the penny image to the Naples's audience. After seeing Astbury's image, Wilkins made an impulse decision and gave an entirely different lecture from the one on proteins he'd been instructed to present. He placed Gosling's early X-ray crystallography image—the "Eureka" image—on show for the audience.

Without mentioning Gosling or Rosalind, Wilkins stated that the image showed that DNA was crystalline in nature. This meant that DNA structure could be discovered by X-ray diffraction and that it definitely had a regular pattern, as Bell's earlier image suggested. Though the exact nature of the pattern was still a mystery, a pattern was something anyone with X-ray diffraction experience and the proper equipment could reveal. Astbury, not knowing that the photo was taken by Gosling, congratulated Wilkins.

None of the official King's DNA team—Rosalind, Gosling, Stokes, or Randall—had a clue that Wilkins would show the lab's proprietary image at the Naples conference. When word of Wilkins's betrayal got back to Randall, he was furious and told Wilkins to leave X-ray diffraction work on DNA to Rosalind. Further, Randall rebuked Wilkins for taking credit for other's work, writing, "I notice you did not make any acknowledgments in your paper to the various people who have helped you."

Rosalind was shocked by Wilkins's public disclosure of others' work, and not only because it violated a scientific code of ethics. He'd revealed Gosling's research results before she and Gosling were certain of what they meant. And by confirming that X-ray crystallography could unlock DNA's secrets, she knew that Wilkins would unleash a worldwide competition to use spectroscopy to complete the analysis of DNA.

Rosalind and Randall were right. From that moment in Naples, the DNA race was on.

After attending the Naples conference, James Watson asked Wilkins if he could join him to work on DNA at King's. Wilkins refused, afraid that Watson might push Wilkins completely out of the way at King's.

Part of the reason for Wilkins's refusal was that he found Watson, only twenty-five at the time, "quite scary" and intimidating. Highly intelligent, Watson had started college at the age of fifteen and was known for his obnoxious, bullying, and socially inept behavior. He had been a contestant at the age of fourteen on a radio show called *Quiz Kids*, losing his match to an eight-year-old he later described with derision as a "little Jewish girl."

Watson instead secured a job at Cavendish College in Cambridge, England, to work with Francis Crick, another molecular biologist. Crick had been at Cavendish since 1949 and was a graduate student pursuing his PhD studying the physical properties of cytoplasm under the direction of molecular biologist Max Perutz and biochemist and crystallographer John Kendrew. Crick had formed a friendship with Wilkins at King's, but in Jim Watson he found a personality that was more complementary to his own.

Crick had, like Watson, a brash, unrestrained nature. The two were known for their raucous laughter, "Crick in a loud bark, Watson in a snuffling snort that showed a lot of his gums." Crick was renowned for saying whatever came into his head, whether he was spouting off on science or philosophy. He preferred (and was regarded as a genius at) looking at the big picture and was slow to work on something as tedious as his doctorate. Watson was only slightly more inclined to rein

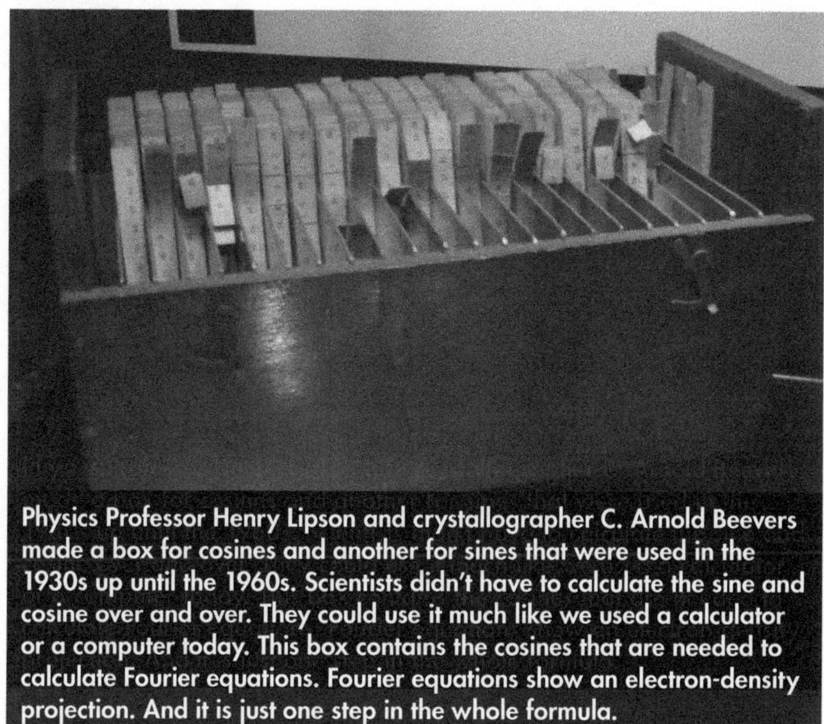

Physics Professor Henry Lipson and crystallographer C. Arnold Beevers made a box for cosines and another for sines that were used in the 1930s up until the 1960s. Scientists didn't have to calculate the sine and cosine over and over. They could use it much like we used a calculator or a computer today. This box contains the cosines that are needed to calculate Fourier equations. Fourier equations show an electron-density projection. And it is just one step in the whole formula.

in rambles. Crick said, "Jim [Watson] and I hit it off immediately, partly because our interests were astonishingly similar and partly, I suspect, because a certain arrogance, a ruthlessness, and an impatience with sloppy thinking comes naturally to both of us."

Most important, Watson and Crick shared the ambition, and the skill sets, that could enable them to uncover the structure for DNA—and win the Nobel Prize.

Also joining the scientific race toward a chemical structure for DNA were Linus Pauling at Caltech in the United States (of whom we'll hear much more) and, of course, Astbury from Leeds. The breakthrough that began with the image Florence Bell had taken in Astbury's lab was enhanced when Wilkins showed rival scientists the more advanced image from King's lab.

By June, scientists from four labs across the globe were in fierce competition to unlock DNA's secrets. But Rosalind was already ahead of everyone.

By July, Rosalind and Gosling, together with mathematician Alec Stokes, had made significant headway on uncovering the structure of DNA. Rosalind carefully measured the X-ray marks on the film, then inserted her measurements into the equations provided by Stokes. Rosalind did this work without the aid of computers, which were still in their infancy. Instead, she wrote her measurements on ordered Beevers-Lipson paper strips. As time-consuming as it was, this technique allowed her to create an exact map of the patterns she observed.

Rosalind's methods of measuring and calculating contrasted with that of the other scientists. Rival labs were trying to short-circuit the process by building physical models and guessing the structure of DNA. Through her exacting calculations, she began to form the hypothesis that DNA structure was helical in form. But she had yet to prove it. Rosalind would accept only a precise X-ray image to confirm her theory.

July 1951, Perutz Conference in Cambridge

Two months after the conference in Naples, molecular biologist Max Perutz called for a conference on the study of protein structures to be held in Cambridge. Rosalind listened in the stifling lecture hall as Wilkins delivered a talk to a group of X-ray experts. Wilkins told the audience, "It seemed that all DNA has the same unique, universal structure which is twisted regularly into a helix."

Rosalind was stunned. He was reckless with others' research. With *her* research. Stokes had told Wilkins that Rosalind had seen a "discernable central 'X' or a 'crossways'" pattern. Wilkins, who had been invited to talk about proteins, did exactly what he'd done in Naples. He prattled on about his time working at the Naples Zoological Society and then segued into revealing Rosalind's unproven hypothesis that the X-ray patterns of DNA showed a helical structure, and Wilkins announced that the King's lab findings proved that the form was a helix.

Rosalind grew increasingly angry as Wilkins not only stole her idea but claimed it as fact. DNA might well be helical in structure, but she knew it was too early to make such a claim. Her fury grew as Wilkins inserted the humorous tales of his adventures at the Zoological Station into her serious science. She felt that by adding those stories into the lecture he was belittling her research. She would not stand for it.

After he finished speaking, Wilkins mingled with the audience members who joined him at the lectern, enthusiastic to hear more about the King's research. He believed his lecture would win back his place as leader of the King's DNA team. Rosalind was waiting for him in the hallway as he left the auditorium. She stopped Wilkins, stepped up close and said in a tone of barely contained anger, "Go back to your microscopes!" Then she turned and left the conference and the speechless Wilkins.

CHAPTER 5

Conference Conundrums

Because her own commitment was total, she was scornful of triflers in science.

—ANNE SAYRE

August–November 26, 1951, King's College Biophysics Lab

Rosalind's determination to prove her hypothesis that the crystalline structure of DNA was a helix was now the heart of her research. But one other piece to the DNA puzzle still had to be understood: its chemical composition. Wilkins was shortly to learn something that would result in finding that puzzle piece. Had Wilkins not been such a difficult colleague, and had Rosalind and Wilkins been better partners, because they had complementary skill sets as Watson and Crick did, they would have brought together these two puzzle pieces earlier than anyone else. And that would have pushed the King's team to the front of the race to uncover the secrets of DNA.

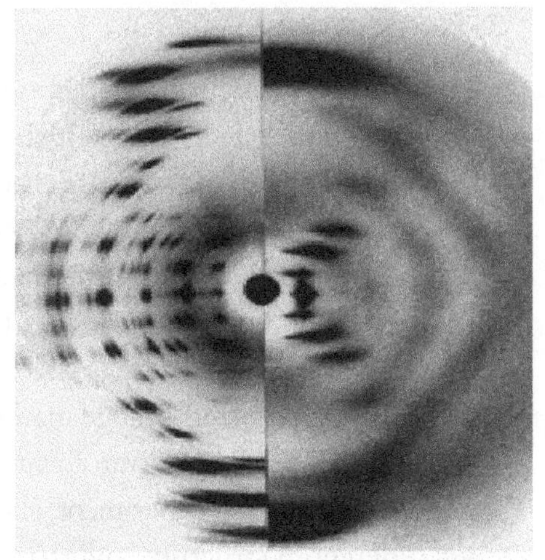

This composite picture shows the X-ray diffraction patterns of the A form and the B form of DNA.

Rosalind's experiments led to ever sharper X-ray crystallography photographs, and she discovered something significant about the patterns she was seeing. She observed that DNA under her analyses did not exhibit one chemical structure but two. She called these two different DNA structures "phases" or "forms" because they were photographed from a single DNA sample at separate times during her long-exposure X-ray imaging. She named the two phases A-DNA and B-DNA.

Her epiphany came from an unexpected factor: the level of humidity in the X-ray chamber during the exposure. This led to an additional observation: The A form was present at lower humidity (and thus called the "dry form") and the B form was present at higher humidity (thus the "wet form").

"Until Rosalind got down to this taking of systematic X-ray diffraction photographs at various humidities no one knew that it was a two-phase structure," Gosling said later. The discovery of two chemical phases (dry and wet) proved to be groundbreaking. Gosling had always had trouble getting his samples of DNA to lie flat, which is why he'd tried using dime-store cement. Rosalind was getting different measurements of the A form each time she ran the experiment. She suspected that the moisture level in the X-ray chamber was to blame for both problems, but she had yet to pin down why.

Even with her discovery of the two phases, or forms, what Rosalind didn't yet know was that the dry A form is also 25 percent shorter and therefore more compact than the wet B form. And A-DNA is both wider and flatter than the B form. The dry A form was therefore simpler to image than the wet B form, but that didn't mean it was easier to interpret, because the X-rays ricocheted off the molecules, causing strange marks on the image. But when she saw that the dry A form transformed into the wet B form in the chamber during the experiment, she could see that the wet form was different in structure, and that any erratic levels of humidity in the equipment's chamber would cause confusing results.

Rosalind realized that exact control of the humidity in the machine was the secret to accurate analysis. A small change would make a dramatic impact. Increasing the humidity in the chamber from 75 percent to 92 percent caused the structure within the sample to change from the A form to the B form. This realization that humidity caused DNA to change form gave Rosalind and Gosling the ability to study the differences between A-DNA and B-DNA in a controlled manner.

Once Rosalind knew how to take more precise measurements, she knew that with the right photograph, she could prove whether the B form, because it was a more reliable and easier to interpret image, was in fact helical. This was the moment that she'd been waiting for—though she had yet to hold photographic proof in her hand.

In August 1951, Rosalind took a much-needed holiday back to France. She met with her old friend Margaret Nance, and they roamed the Brittany countryside. By bike, she visited other friends in the Dordogne. Her holiday reminded her of her Paris years, and she grew nostalgic for the lab experience she'd had there.

But while she was away, Wilkins once again inserted himself into her DNA research, asking Stokes to make a mathematical prediction of how a helical structure might look in an X-ray image. Wilkins left Rosalind a note about Stokes's results, which she found on her desk on her return to King's. Useful or not, his interference was unwanted, and Rosalind was furious. This was not her sought-after collaboration. It felt like an intrusion.

Her anger at Wilkins simmered at length, partly because Wilkins was away when she returned. Wilkins had left King's to attend the annual Gordon Research Conference, a prestigious invitation-only retreat-style gathering of chemists and biophysicists. Rosalind had not been invited, but Wilkins was thrilled to be so honored, despite the demand, for the third time, from Randall that Wilkins not discuss the lab's DNA work.

At the conference, Wilkins learned of the research results of Erwin Chargaff, a Ukrainian American chemist. Chargaff had long suspected that DNA was made up of only four nucleotides and these nucleotides were the basis for all genes, but his findings had seemed too simple for such a complex system.

With chromatograph technology, Chargaff and his cohort had been able to count the number of nucleotides in DNA samples. Within each strand of DNA, he found uniform amounts of adenine (A) and thymine (T). And he found equal amounts of cytosine (C) and guanine (G). The A/T nucleotide bases and the C/G nucleotide bases were building blocks for the long, complicated sequences of DNA. Chargaff called these building blocks "base-pairings."

Chargaff then compared human DNA with the DNA of different species—chickens, grasshoppers, and sea urchins—and discovered that the makeup of DNA differs from one species to another. The percentages of A/T and G/C in a living organism determine the species. Chargaff found that he could tell if a DNA sample was human or chicken, grasshopper or sea urchin, simply by the proportion of the base pairs. This groundbreaking research was one missing piece of the DNA puzzle: its chemical composition.

Wilkins believed that Chargaff's findings would shed new light on and possibly reinterpret Rosalind's work. When he returned to King's, he went straight to Rosalind, suggesting that they collaborate. But before Wilkins had the chance to even open the discussion of the Chargaff findings with her, Rosalind, still seething about his working with Stokes while she was on holiday, exploded, "How dare you interpret my data for me!" Her outburst startled Wilkins, and he backed away.

He said, "Her air of cool superiority—a look I have never forgotten—temporarily undermined my self-confidence, and gave me a brief feeling of panic." Wilkins felt as if the air in the room had grown cold, and he left, having never told her about Chargaff's discovery.

"If you believed what you were saying," Gosling said about their exchanges, "you had to argue very strongly with Rosalind if she thought you were wrong, whereas Maurice would simply shut up." And retreat. Wilkins's nonresponses to Rosalind provoked both her contempt, and in this case, her misery at her situation at King's.

Not long after this confrontation, Rosalind arrived for dinner at her brother Colin's house in tears. Wilkins had thought she was enraged, but she told Colin that she felt betrayed. She told him that as exciting as her science was and as happy as she was having family nearby, she was considering leaving King's. "I came back from my holiday to the blackest of crises in the lab," Rosalind wrote later, "which took all my energy. I think seriously of [going] back to Paris if Paris will have me."

Knowing that DNA research would benefit from their collaboration, Randall tried to broker a truce between Rosalind and Wilkins. Randall ordered Rosalind to concentrate on studying the A form of DNA while Wilkins would concentrate on the B form. Rosalind took the Signer DNA sample and her reconfigured equipment. Wilkins was left with the less workable thymus sample and his microscopes. With his limited tools and sample, and his inability to speak up with Rosalind, Wilkins was even more isolated in the department. He felt misused by Randall's directive, saying, "His manner of telling us did not help matters: he said he wanted to be fair to both of us, and that made me feel like a naughty child."

Wilkins turned to his friend Francis Crick at the Cavendish lab for advice. Wilkins told Crick that he wanted to try to reach out to Rosalind. Crick's advice was to be more friendly toward Rosalind. Wilkins decided he would try "taking her out to dinner and giving her a few drinks and trying to find out more about her troubles. I always liked the girl."

Despite their personality clash, by all observations of onlookers in the lab and elsewhere, Wilkins did like Rosalind quite a lot. Vittorio Luzzati believed that "Wilkins was fiercely attracted by Rosalind, and that all the problems at King's can be traced to this." Yet, as Luzzati added, "Wilkins wasn't a strong man, and Rosalind disliked weak men."

Raymond Gosling said, "Rosalind was attractive and maybe their mutual animosity had something to do with this supposed mutual attraction . . . this was generally believed to be true among the people at King's."

"All the students," added Margaret North, "who observed things from a little bit of a distance were convinced that Wilkins was in love with Rosalind and that she had rejected him, and that this was the basis for their animosity."

Decoding DNA

At the end of the 1800s, a biochemist named Albrecht Kossel (1853–1927) identified four basic chemical components in DNA and called them nucleobases. They are adenine (A), thymine (T), cytosine (C), and guanine (G). A nucleobase plus a 5-carbon sugar plus a phosphate group make a unit called a nucleotide. With just four letters, DNA should be easy to read or understand, yet it isn't. In the 1800s all the rules of DNA grammar had not been uncovered and understood.

Erwin Chargaff (1905–2002) found a way to separate and color Kossel's nucleobases from the rest of the DNA molecule. The method, called chromatography, is what allowed him to determine that the strands of DNA contain

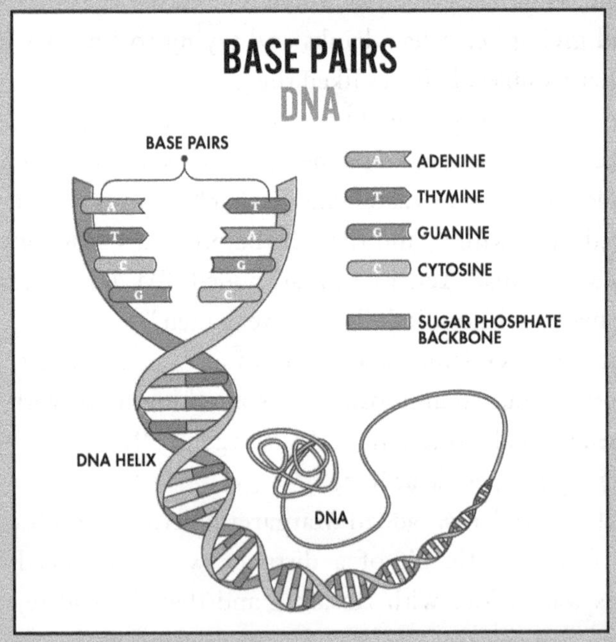

roughly equal amounts of A and T as well as equal amounts of C and G. Along with his grad assistant, he named the C/T base pairs pyrimidines, and the A/G base pairs purines. The amounts of bases vary from species to species, but do not vary between individuals of the same species.

Organism	**A base** (%)	**T base** (%)	**G base** (%)	**C base** (%)
Humans	30.9	29.4	19.9	19.8
Chickens	28.8	29.2	20.5	21.5
Grasshoppers	29.3	29.3	20.5	20.7
Sea urchins	32.8	32.1	26.0	25.7

Loosely speaking, a gene in DNA is like a word in English. As each word holds a specific meaning, each gene represents a specific trait. A gene is an incredibly long sequence of nucleotides along a DNA string. The string of nucleotides also varies in length—each can vary from 500 to 2.3 million nucleotides laced together. Nucleotides are linked by the sugar of one nucleotide and the phosphate group of the next forming the sugar phosphate backbone of DNA. This sequence determines a characteristic for an organism—from eye color to height, freckles to a bent pinkie, or explains someone's ability to roll their tongue. The order of nucleotides in this DNA string represents the blueprint for that organism whether human, animal, plant, or bacteria.

Today, the entire human genome has been sequenced and there are around three billion base pairs that have also been decoded.

Anne Sayre asked Crick if he knew why Rosalind and Wilkins had got on so badly. Crick answered promptly, "All of us have always believed it was sexual, purely sexual. We all think Maurice was in love with her."

Whether his motives were romantic or scientific, Wilkins was socially inept, especially with women, and perhaps particularly with Rosalind. His approach to patching things up with her by asking her out after his discussion with Crick did not go over well.

He made his attempt when Rosalind was again sitting on the floor under her X-ray equipment sorting out a problem with the electrical wiring. She was frustrated and deep into her task when Wilkins wandered into the small lab space and hovered over her. Her white lab coat was dirty from the grimy floor, the lab was hot, and her focus was on the mess of wires dangling around her. She didn't want to be bothered by Wilkins, especially when she was trying to concentrate. She treated him pleasantly enough but was relieved when, after a few oddly noncommittal remarks about her work, he left her to finish her job. Rosalind was completely unaware of his aborted attempt to invite her out.

Wilkins went back to Crick. Watson was present when Wilkins arrived at Cavendish. Wilkins launched into an insulting tirade about Rosalind. She was "sprawled out on the floor of her lab dressed in a smudged lab coat," Wilkins said, and added that she suffered from offensive "body odor." Rosalind did not fit the image Wilkins had of a young woman he would invite to dinner, saying that he "objected to the very idea of sitting down to dinner with Franklin in her present smelly state." As far as he was concerned, there would be no more attempts to win Rosalind's favor.

He then betrayed her further by sharing with the two other

John T. Randall uses a microscope in the lab.

scientists—scientists in a rival lab who also wanted to uncover DNA's secrets—what he knew about Rosalind's work at King's. He blamed her for his loss of the Signer samples and use of King's X-ray equipment. Wilkins told Watson and Crick that, regardless of what Randall wanted, Wilkins would continue to work on DNA. In other words, Wilkins—snubbed, usurped, belittled, and thwarted in his affections—would do anything to stay in the DNA race.

November 21, 1951, the Colloquium at King's College

Shortly after Wilkins's social failure with Rosalind, Randall scheduled an internal colloquium for King's scientists to take inventory of the X-ray diffraction and DNA work happening in their lab. Wilkins privately kept Watson and Crick informed about the colloquium and let them know that Rosalind would be speaking about her research. Watson asked if he could attend, and Wilkins extended an invitation with the excuse that since both institutions were funded by the Medical Research Council (MRC), Watson's presence was perfectly fine.

Fifteen people attended the colloquium, including the three speakers: Wilkins, Stokes, and Rosalind. Wilkins gave the same presentation he had given at the Perutz conference and again brought up his yet unproven belief in DNA's helical structure. He also shared for the first time publicly what he'd learned from Chargaff about the chemical composition of DNA and the ACTG base pairs. Stokes spoke about the math behind DNA's repeating structures. Rosalind shared her discovery of the effects of humidity, and another recent observation, that the phosphate base pairs were on the *outside* of the molecule. She also revealed her hypothesis of a helical structure to DNA, but unlike Wilkins, she wouldn't confirm it because her work was incomplete.

Watson, a tall, disheveled young man, was easy to notice in the audience. Comically, he tried to hide behind a newspaper pretending that he wasn't paying attention, and as a point of personal pride, he took no notes. But because he didn't understand the science well enough to remember the details from Rosalind's lecture, when Watson ran into Crick at Paddington Station the morning after the colloquium, he explained Rosalind's lecture all wrong. Among other mistakes, Watson told Crick that Rosalind had found that the phosphate pairs were *inside* the molecule. Using the nickname that Rosalind hated, he said incorrectly, "Rosy did not give a hoot about the creation of the helical theory." Possibly influenced by Wilkins's earlier descriptions, Watson also insulted her appearance, saying that she was unfeminine.

From Watson's information, or rather misinformation, Crick performed new calculations and determined that there were only a few possible structures for DNA with centrally placed phosphates. Crick assured Watson that he would have a DNA model (the physical model that so many of the researchers then favored) within a week. But instead of giving Cavendish an advantage, Watson's misunderstanding put them on the wrong track. Cavendish was building the wrong model of DNA structure—a structure that Rosalind had right.

CHAPTER 6

Trip to Cavendish's Room 103

She had a capacity for tact, but she was also extremely honest, and if tact and honesty conflicted on any important matter, the honesty won.

—ANNE SAYRE

November 27, 1951, Cavendish College in London

Rosalind looked with scorn at Watson and Crick's physical model of DNA structure, and bluntly said, "You're wrong."

A week had passed since the King's colloquium. The Cavendish team, having built the model based on Watson's misinformation and Crick's math analysis, wanted to show Wilkins what they had accomplished. Crick expected Wilkins to come to Cavendish right away and arrive alone. But Wilkins acted aloof and said he "might make it sometime within the week." Later, Wilkins reflected that he "did not like the idea of being in a race with Cambridge." But it was a race, and that reality resulted in a strange turn of events.

Because he believed Rosalind's colloquium talk had been the inspiration for the Watson-Crick model, John Kendrew, an administrator at Cavendish who also worked for MRC, insisted that all the King's scientists working on DNA be invited to the Cavendish unveiling. Kendrew wanted everything aboveboard.

Rosalind knew that Watson and Crick were heavily invested in the notion of a helix structure but lacked evidence. She was still analyzing her data, and she was the only one with crystallographic images. She was skeptical that the Cavendish team could have created a successful helical prototype without images and analysis. When she received her invitation to the Cavendish lab for the unveiling, she, like Kendrew, suspected that whatever their model was that they'd based it partly on the results she'd presented at the colloquium.

She would prove to be right but with a twist.

Rosalind, Gosling, Wilkins, research assistant Bill Fraser, and Bill Seeds traveled by train to Cambridge. It was a long trip, almost 50 miles (81 km) from the lab at King's in London. During the journey, Rosalind did her best to ignore Wilkins who, in turn, actively ignored Rosalind, as he had ever since the failed attempt to invite her out. Instead of the usual bus ride from the train station to Cavendish, Wilkins decided to grab a cab. Rosalind decided she would rather take the bus than sit squashed in next to Wilkins and the other men.

Once the scientists had regrouped at Cavendish, Rosalind listened impatiently to the introductions and obligatory chit-chat. When, at last, Crick began the meeting with an attempt to dazzle the King's scientists with his calculations, he positioned his presentation as sharing new information, but it wasn't new to the researchers from King's.

Surprising everyone, Wilkins listened only for a brief time before he interrupted the proceedings to point out that Crick was reiterating what the King's team had produced. Further, Wilkins stated that Stokes had already made Crick's same calculations, adding that Stokes had "produced the theory on a small sheet of paper," implying Stokes's superior math skills. For once, Rosalind was pleased by Wilkins's protective stance of King's work and Stokes's math.

Crick changed course, and he and Watson unveiled their model. To Rosalind it looked like an inaccurate mess of wire and metal, with clips holding everything together. She stood, even though they were still mid-presentation. Maybe she was partly inspired by Wilkins's comments. More likely, she was impatient with the poor science before her. All eyes were on her as she cataloged the Cavendish model's inaccuracies, annihilated their theories, and deflated Watson and Crick's hopes for glory with her litany of facts.

Rosalind first brought up the issue of water content. Watson had heard in her colloquium talk that the A form changed to the B form, but they were missing the mechanism to make that happen—water. The change in form would only be possible with a higher water content than the one they presented. The tenfold increase in the amount of water needed meant that the possible variations of any DNA model increased substantially. Rosalind pointed out that the Cavendish crew had overlooked an inordinate number of possible models.

The second issue Rosalind raised was their theory that charged magnesium ions were responsible for holding the phosphate groups together. In the Cavendish model, magnesium ions would be encased by water molecules and water would neutralize any ionic charge. Neutralized ions and water could

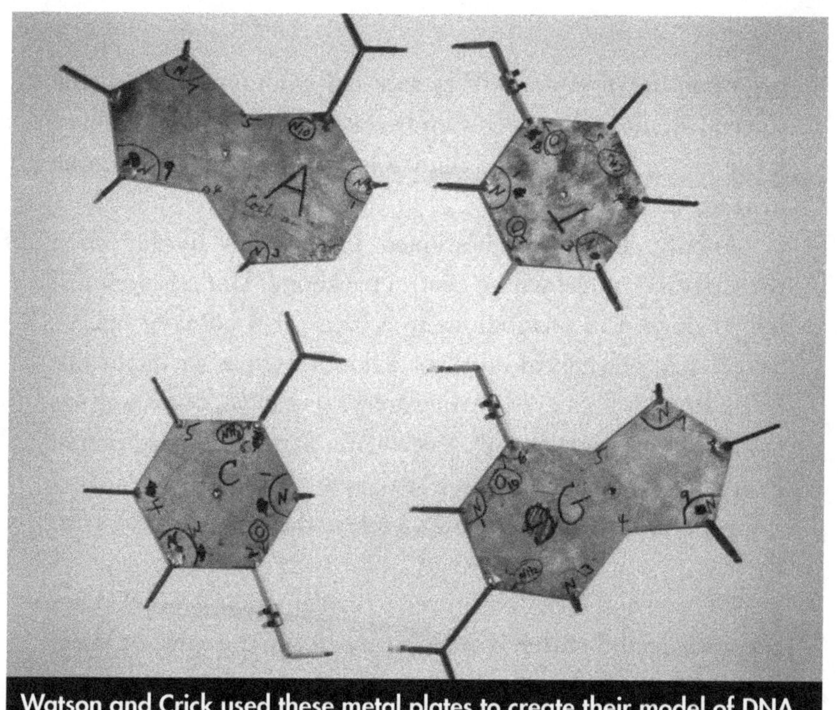

Watson and Crick used these metal plates to create their model of DNA.

not act as a bonding agent. Rosalind finished this point with a declaration that ions could not take on the role of the "kingpins of a tight structure." In other words, charged ions could not take on the role of holding the phosphate groups together. The desire of the Cavendish team (Crick a biologist and neuroscientist and Watson a biologist) to be the first to discover the secrets of DNA made them rush and make a basic chemistry mistake that Rosalind, as a chemist, recognized at once.

Third, Rosalind raised the issue of the structure that Watson had misremembered. Rosalind and Gosling's X-ray diffraction patterns showed that the phosphate groups were on the outside around the central core containing the rest of the nucleotides. Watson and Crick's model placed the phosphate groups on the inside of the DNA molecule, at the core, the opposite of Rosalind's established findings. At this, the Cavendish men were deeply embarrassed. Watson should have taken notes at the colloquium. Or Crick should have gone instead.

Finally, Rosalind questioned Cavendish's display of a three-strand model with a central backbone. Her research had boiled down the possibilities to a "2, 3 or 4 co-axial nucleic acid chains per helical unit," or a double, triple, or quadruple helix. Rosalind believed a triple helix was *possible*, but it was too bold an assumption for her. Watson and Crick had been caught gambling: This was science, not a game of cards.

Rosalind faced the men and asked them, where was their data?

Watson and Crick scrambled to explain their process. They acknowledged that they'd failed to appreciate the value of imaging and thought that building models was a useful strategy. But their model had been entirely wrong, and Rosalind made that clear. Adding insult to injury, Watson and Crick's model of DNA looked as if they had been playing with Tinkertoys—a 1914-era toy building set of wooden spools and dowels that could be connected into different forms. There wasn't much difference between what the Cavendish scientists had produced and the toy itself. Watson said later, "The idea of using tinker-toy-like models to solve biological structures was clearly a last resort."

And Crick admitted, "We made asses of ourselves."

In the moment, Crick tried to pivot to the science. But something in the air had shifted. Crick and Watson were forced to propose that King's and Cavendish work together. Rosalind immediately quashed that possibility. She knew now that Watson had taken her work from the colloquium and tried to make it appear as their own. And not only had he copied her work, but he'd copied it wrong. Work together, when she was sure the Cavendish team didn't know what they were doing? Not a chance.

Rosalind's counterpoints to their model were all accurate, but the one that probably hurt Cavendish the most that day was their gross underestimation of water in the model. Watson had undervalued Rosalind's scientific expertise and overvalued his own abilities.

On the train back to King's, Rosalind felt vindicated. She'd shown the men that she knew what she was talking about. But she found it disheartening to see how desperate Watson and Crick had been to be the first to demystify DNA. She could not understand why it was so important for them to win the DNA race that they were willing to not only steal but also misinterpret her research. To her, the pursuit of science was its own reward.

None of Rosalind's actions at that meeting were meant to be hostile. Gosling said, "I knew that she wasn't an unkind person at all and that what she was concerned with was the problem, and personalities didn't come into it." Nevertheless, he added, "This didn't win friends and influence people."

Word of Cavendish's poorly constructed model traveled through Cambridge faster than the train back to London. Lawrence Bragg, the head of the Cavendish lab, wanted answers as to why any team at Cavendish was working on the structure of DNA rather than their assigned projects, and especially why grad student Crick wasn't working on his doctorate. At King's, Randall was also incensed. Wilkins clearly had ignored his instructions to leave DNA alone. Bragg and Randall, who were old acquaintances and colleagues, had a heated conversation that afternoon. During their phone call, they decided that Watson and Crick, in particular, and Cavendish, in general, would no longer work on DNA. Bragg delivered the message to Watson and Crick that DNA research would be solely done at King's.

A few days later, Rosalind watched the delivery of a box to her biophysics lab at King's. The delivery was from Cavendish. The box was filled with Watson and Crick's model manufacturing parts: bits of metal, wire, molds, and metal jigs to create spheres. Watson and Crick had been given a cease and desist, and the Cavendish team had to dispose of their model. Was this delivery a gesture of goodwill? As Rosalind wasn't inclined to build models, she set the box aside. She had her own equipment, her own methods, and she didn't have any need for Cavendish's spare parts. "Rosalind didn't like the idea of building a model," Gosling said, ". . . because—as she said—how the hell do you prove that that's the unique solution?"

The research to uncover the crystalline structure of DNA was finally fully in Rosalind's domain at King's. And the structure would not be understood by using Tinkertoys but by precise scientific processes.

CHAPTER 7

A Disappointing Trip to Paris

She developed a physical stoicism which sometimes proved extreme.

—ANNE SAYRE

December 1951–January 1952, Paris

Fierce competition was in the air. Labs across the United States and Europe were battling to be the first to crack the structure of DNA. Scientists hoarded information as they coveted being first to this groundbreaking discovery. They all yearned for the Nobel Prize.

An agreement to control research between labs—especially for something this monumental—was rare. Yet after the flawed model release, Watson and Crick were reassigned to the outskirts of DNA research. But Wilkins was caught up in the fever of the DNA race. He decided that he would become a conduit of information between his own lab and Cavendish despite Randall's and Bragg's edict. He excused this betrayal later, saying, "We [King's and Cavendish] ought to have seen that there was a real need for collaboration." But rather than a true collaboration, Wilkins began a quiet alliance with Watson and Crick, enabling them to continue their hunt for the structure of DNA.

In late 1951, Rosalind decided to clear her head and gain perspective away from King's. Her exasperation with the level of competition and the belittling of her work from Watson, Crick, and Wilkins was reaching the boiling point. Rosalind told Anne Sayre that "the middle and senior people are positively repulsive, and it is they who set the general tone [at King's]. I've got myself organised so that I hardly ever see any of them, which makes things better but distinctly boring." Rosalind longed to revive her Paris experience of friendship, kinship, and collaboration. She returned to the city for a week in January 1952. Deep down, she realized that the goal of her trip was to assess if she needed more than a breather. She was wondering whether she should leave the nonsense around the DNA race in England and move back to Paris.

She also wanted Vittorio Luzzati's opinion about next steps for her project at King's. After sharing a few of the early images she had taken in the lab, the two talked about strategies for analyzing the scattered dots on her photos. Luzzati reminded Rosalind of a technique called the Patterson method. When it came to measuring the distance between atoms in a crystal to determine its structure, the laborious Patterson method was considered the gold standard within the crystallography industry. Invented in the 1930s by a crystallographer named Arthur L. Patterson, the technique excelled at studying small

Women in Science in the 1950s

Women have made countless contributions to science. But they faced many obstacles to do so. Colleges generally didn't admit women until the late 1800s and early 1900s. Degrees started to be awarded to woman slowly; it was not a universal change—colleges and universities varied wildly on when they started offering women undergraduate and PhD designations.

Dorothy Hodgkin in her lab

In 1903, Marie Curie was the first woman to win a Nobel Prize. During WWII, opportunities for women in science research increased and kept increasing throughout the 1900s. In the 1950s, notable women in science included computer scientist Grace Hopper, radiobiologist Alma Howard, physicist Chien-Shiung Wu, and geochemist Katsuko Saruhashi. Rosalind's contemporary and friend, Dorothy Hodgkin, won the 1964 Nobel Prize in Chemistry for her work in that decade and in the 1940s. No woman was a Nobel laureate during the 1950s. Between Marie Curie's 1903 Nobel and 1960 only two women won Nobels in the sciences: Gerty Cori (1947, Physiology or Medicine) and Irene Joliot-Curie (1935, Chemistry).

Today many initiatives exist to ensure science, technology, engineering, and math skills are introduced and nurtured early for all individuals, and the number of Nobels increasingly awarded to women reflects that new reality.

molecules of organic material. The technique was well suited to Rosalind's unique skill set. Luzatti may have advised Rosalind that "it's what a crystallographer would do," referring to using the Patterson method, and that would have suited her dedication to good science.

Luzzati also offered Rosalind a way back to Paris: She could work on liquids with him. But when she considered it, she thought moving back to Paris would be taking a big step backward in her career. She knew that her work on the structure of DNA was heading in the right direction.

And Luzzati and her old boss (and wishful romantic partner) Jacques Mering were worlds apart in welcoming her back. While Luzzati was open, Mering was dismissive and held it against Rosalind that she had left to go to King's in the first place. He refused her request to lend his name to the papers based on their joint research, which in academia is tantamount to rejecting the quality of the science. More painfully, he was blunt and unfriendly toward her when they met.

Her mentor Adrienne Weill watched this interaction with Mering with concern, knowing that Rosalind still had feelings for Mering, and worrying about Rosalind's emotional state as well as her professional future. But alas, a return for Rosalind to work in Paris was not possible, given Mering's harsh rebuff.

England was moving into a new era in the early 1950s. Rosalind was only just back from Paris when King George VI died in his sleep following surgery for a long illness, following which twenty-seven-year-old Princess Elizabeth ascended to the throne. The war was fading into memory. The bomb crater on the King's campus was filled, and shortages began to abate.

Rosalind reflected with regret that she wouldn't be moving back to Paris. "I suspect," she said sadly to Anne Sayre, "that I enjoyed being a more interesting person in France than I am in England."

But Luzzati's mention of the Patterson technique prompted Rosalind to consider a possible way to escape the suffocating atmosphere at King's. On her return to London, she went directly to Birkbeck College to see John D. Bernal, the head of the Physics Department there. One of Bernal's collaborators, Carolyn Cohen, was a renowned expert in the Patterson method. Rosalind asked Bernal if she could join his group, leaving King's. Bernal gave Rosalind a tentative yes—but meanwhile, she had to return to King's and keep her plans quiet until the move could be secured.

Right after her return to the lab, Randall asked Rosalind to chronicle her previous year's work at King's. This report was for the benefit of the Turner and Newall Fellowship Committee, the institution that supplied the funding for her King's fellowship. Rosalind detailed her assembly of the lab systems, and she related how she had created the critical humid environment in which she could x-ray DNA. She credited Wilkins for procuring the Signer sample. She also chronicled the discovery of taking the crystalline state (the dry A-DNA form) of the sample to the paracrystalline (wet B-DNA form), and she shared that the length of the fibers changed with hydration.

Most important, she suggested that there could be two, three, or even four chains within her helical unit. Finally, she explained her November 1951 colloquium presentation, including the symmetry she found in the A-DNA form as well as relevant dimensions. These were the measurements, along with the role that water played, that Watson did not remember when he tried to relay Rosalind's lecture to Crick.

Rosalind submitted her report on February 7, 1952. It provides the most complete window into her hypothesis of a helical structure to DNA, though whether it was double, triple, or quadruple she wasn't ready to say.

Rosalind's sense of isolation at King's might have lessened if she'd found even one sympathetic mentor. A good possibility existed in renowned organic chemist Dorothy Hodgkin. Hodgkin was Bernal's former lover (before her marriage), and she was a future Nobel laureate and was already highly respected and accepted despite her gender. Rosalind took a chance and contacted the older scientist.

Rosalind carried several of her photographs to Hodgkin's lab at Oxford, and Hodgkin told Rosalind that the photos "were the best she had ever seen." But when Rosalind began to propose the ideas about DNA structure she had formed from the images, Hodgkin interrupted and told her that two of Rosalind's three explanations were inconsistent with her data. Rosalind left the meeting feeling it had soured any possible further collaboration with a woman scientist who might have been a true colleague.

Her isolation, her antagonistic relationship with Wilkins, her dismissive attitude toward some at King's whom she considered having not "a good brain among them," and the loss of a return to Paris led to Rosalind's growing reputation in the lab as moody and difficult. She was often seen storming around the lab, eyes blazing.

Adrienne Weill said,

> *Rosalind's unhappiness at King's sprang not from a personal conflict with Wilkins or anyone, but simply from the general atmosphere at King's which was cold, dreary, antiwoman, and not intellectually serious. Rosalind couldn't*

understand why the people at King's were so lackadaisical about their work, so unexcited by it, so perfunctory and that this sort of attitude was of all things calculated to rouse Rosalind's contempt. Long before any friction rose between Rosalind and Wilkins, Rosalind was deeply irritated with the whole institution; later, Wilkins seemed simply to personify the chilly feebleness of King's at its highest degree.

Despite Rosalind's scientific achievements at King's, a break was coming.

Birkbeck was her option. Bernal was respected for his research of biological molecules, and he'd started using X-ray crystallography in the 1920s at the time when the fields of biology and physics didn't yet comingle. Bernal was a known Communist, but that didn't influence Rosalind one way or another. She told Sayre that he was a brilliant scientist and that was the type of person she wanted to work with. Although he wasn't working on DNA, Bernal was working on viruses, and Rosalind considered both subjects worthy of serious research. Moving to Birkbeck could take her on a new, equally significant scientific journey.

Although a job at Birkbeck would be a downgrade from King's College, Rosalind believed that the Birkbeck crowd might be more to her liking than those at King's. It was a night school for working people, therefore a harkening back to her father's volunteer after-hours teaching experiences. The students at Birkbeck were there because they wanted to learn, a trait Rosalind respected. And many members of the Birkbeck team were Jewish. As she put it, "King's had neither foreigners nor Jews." The insular, largely male, mostly white, Protestant English cohort that surrounded her at King's made her feel alien.

After hearing Rosalind's complaints, Sayre wrote that if Rosalind were ever to murder someone at King's, Sayre would "fly over as a character witness and swear it was justifiable homicide."

But before she could leave King's, Rosalind had to complete the work that she'd started there, and that would lead to the most significant discovery in the history of DNA research.

CHAPTER 8

Photo 51

She had discovered young . . . the true framework of her future. She had no doubts about her intention to do science and modern science is done in professional terms.

—ANNE SAYRE

May 1952, King's College Biophysics Lab

Back at work in the spring of 1952, months before she moved to Birkbeck, Rosalind was still perfecting the microscopic camera that she and Gosling had designed. The fabrication was being completed in King's technical workshop, which had "liberated" parts from German laboratories after the war and so were able to fashion new equipment. Rosalind was so involved in tweaking her camera that one technician recalled her coming into the lab at night in evening dress to make a quick adjustment before swirling away, and thought he'd been "visited by a creature from another planet."

Rosalind's intense ability to focus on complex topics at all times was foreign to many of her colleagues, and one of her obstacles was her gender. Geoffrey Brown, a King's graduate student in physics who witnessed Rosalind's tenure there, wrote, "One of the most invidious and damaging anti-woman aspects of King's was that the workshop was uncooperative about producing equipment for women—that the workshop could not be dealt with by women at all, and that any woman in the place had to do all her dealings through some male agent."

Fortunately, Gosling was on Rosalind's team. The photographs that she and Gosling took that spring were so sharp that Dorothy Hodgkin told Rosalind that it actually "might be possible to work out the space group of the crystal"—or determine whether the crystalline structure was indeed helical and whether the helix was double, triple, or quadruple. Rosalind was almost certain that the B form of DNA was a helix of some kind. But regarding the A form, despite Hodgkin's assurances that the answer might be found, Rosalind, possibly burned by her earlier interaction with Hodgkin, wasn't ready to commit. As always, she required the absolute scientific proof.

On May 1, 1952, Rosalind and Gosling set up their camera for a long exposure of a single DNA fiber at the very close range of 15 mm. After waiting through nearly one hundred hours of exposure and after the crystalline A form transformed into the paracrystalline B form, as it had in their previous attempts to capture the structure, they produced an image.

Those one hundred hours had been tense. Rosalind bubbled hydrogen gas through salt solutions and flooded the gas into a chamber containing her meticulously prepared specimen. The chamber was leaking so much that Gosling worried the two of them would blow themselves up and, as they were in a windowless basement lab on the campus, take half of King's

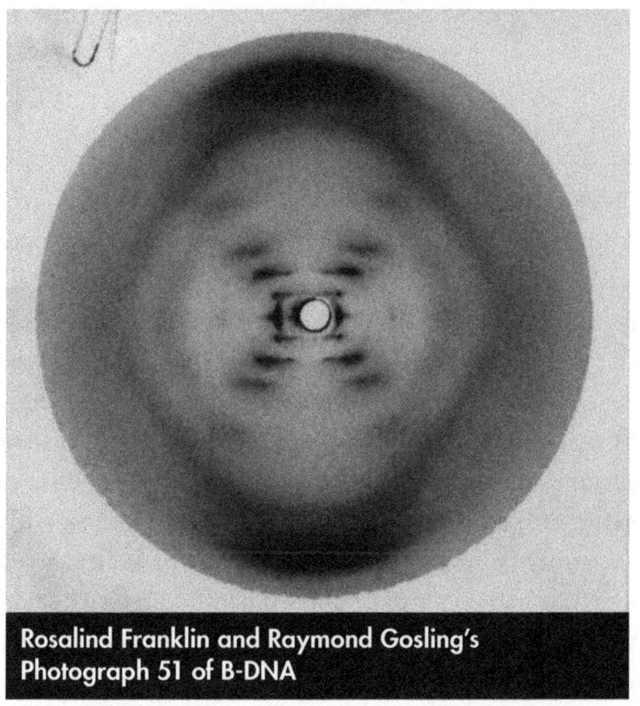

Rosalind Franklin and Raymond Gosling's Photograph 51 of B-DNA

College with them. It was a reasonable worry. One spark from the 50,000 volts on the old, exposed X-ray tube was all it would take to ignite the hydrogen gas.

But after those one hundred hours of exposure, they had a photograph that would become one of the most important made in the history of science. She and Gosling produced a clear image of the B form of DNA. Rosalind scanned it with her usual precision and her unusual ability to envision a two-dimensional picture in three dimensions. The photograph showed a distinct X, with black stripes that radiated from its center. The space between the arms of the X were blank, and Rosalind concluded that the B form was almost certainly a helix.

She numbered the image of that B-form DNA fiber "Photograph 51," and it would play a critical role in the DNA story, and in Rosalind's story too.

While Rosalind was sure that the B form image was groundbreaking, she still wanted to answer an important question concerning DNA's A form—whether it, too, was helical. She didn't jump to the conclusion that because the B form was helical, the A form must be as well. In fact, she wondered whether her experiment suggested that the A form was asymmetrical.

When she ran into Francis Crick at a meeting in Cambridge, she mentioned that she thought the A form might be asymmetrical. Rather than discussing her notions with her, Crick, firmly believing now that DNA had a helical structure (although he had no proof), belittled her. Later, Crick said, "I'm afraid we always used to adopt—let's say a *patronising* attitude towards her." He admitted that this attitude prompted Rosalind to be defensive.

For Rosalind, being defensive meant devoting herself to doing more analyses, collecting more data, and applying more rigorous techniques to her crystallography. Crick and Watson were interested in success. Rosalind Franklin was interested in science.

Rosalind felt fortunate to work with Gosling. He matched her enthusiasm for the research. Their Photo 51 brought true clarity to the structure of DNA in at least the B form. This image closed the gap from Florence Bell's image fifteen years prior. But great images require great analysis. Rosalind had previously used the Patterson method to research the microstructures of coal, charcoal, and graphite. With the suggestion from Luzzati, she decided it was worth the tedious effort to apply the Patterson method to both A-DNA and B-DNA. The images she'd made showed the right amount of diffraction data, clarity, and a repeating structure—a pattern.

Rosalind and Gosling set about to study the electron density, or packing, of each individual atom to come up with a number to be used in their calculations. This would be repeated for all the scatter dots in an image. The end goal, if they applied the Patterson method correctly, was a complete vector allowing them to visualize the distance between every atom in relation to every other atom in one DNA image. Rosalind believed that this method, rather than model-building as the Watson-Crick team had done, was the road to visualizing the structure of DNA.

But she needed to decide to which form she would first apply the Patterson method. She contemplated her images of the dry crystalline A-DNA form and the hydrated B-DNA form. The A form was shorter and more compact than the seemingly complicated hydrated B form, making it easier to x-ray. The B form as seen in Photo 51 was clear and distinct. From these data, Rosalind decided that since the dry A form was harder to interpret, it would be better to apply the Patterson method to A.

Additionally, she liked the amount of diffraction detail and resolution on the A-DNA image. Other crystallographers, including Bell and Astbury, had struggled with too *little* diffraction data in their images, and Bernal and Hodgkin had too *much* diffraction data, with patterns consisting of thousands of reflections. But Rosalind felt she could thread the middle with the right hydration in the X-ray chamber.

Unsure whether the photograph of the B-DNA form showed a two-, three-, or four-chain helix and now set on analyzing the A-DNA form, Rosalind set Photo 51 aside, placing it inside her desk drawer.

CHAPTER 9

The Patterson Method and Memorial Card for DNA

She could stick to her guns with immovable stubbornness when she thought she was right because no matter of importance could be lightly abandoned; that would have been betrayal.

—ANNE SAYRE

June 1952, King's College Biophysics Lab and Cavendish College

Rosalind and Gosling set to work using the Patterson method on the A form of DNA. She believed that to obtain an accurate Patterson map, they could not overlook a single diffraction spot. Their outcome would only be as good as their data collection.

A complication was that their X-ray images were two-dimensional. The darker the dots on their images, the more atoms in the crystal structure. They'd need to determine the angle for every scattered X-ray in their photograph. That meant the Patterson method could only provide the relative positions of atoms within a single plane of their crystal. Evaluating one X-ray image would not give a three-dimensional picture of the molecule. Rosalind would need to move the molecule through hundreds of different rotations by hand. Each rotation required a new X-ray. She and Gosling had to calculate perhaps thousands of vector lengths. If they could calculate the seemingly infinite number of combinations and locations of these atoms, then they would have the structure of DNA.

Gosling brought oranges to the lab to help them think in terms of spheres. He recalled a relaxed afternoon when he and Rosalind were having a hard time with the calculations, and they ended up eating the oranges and then threw orange peels at each other. "There was quite a lot of orange peel on the floor," Gosling recounted, laughing. "And it was great fun!" Gosling was up for this meticulous if sometimes tedious work with Rosalind. Also, he liked her. "She could be very proper," Gosling said, but "she was very, at times, very relaxed to work with."

Gosling respected the level of effort because no one had yet measured DNA with such accuracy. If Watson and Crick had taken Photo 51 themselves, they wouldn't bother with the hard work involved in the Patterson method. James Watson confessed that he didn't grasp the technique. Francis Crick rejected using the method for organic molecules, thus avoiding the burdensome calculations. But Rosalind, with Gosling, knew they needed the data to prove any hypothesis.

In June 1952 Rosalind was invited to speak in Yugoslavia about her coal research, and needing a break, she accepted the invitation. She had met with Bernal again at Birkbeck and said, "He will take me at any time if Randall agrees, but I've decided it would be bad politics to talk to Randall just before going away for a month, so that's a pleasure in store for me when I get back." She was done with King's, but still had months to go before she could make the break. So, after a successful lecture in Zagreb, Croatia, she made a vacation of the trip. She hiked in the French Alps, and passed through Venice, Italy, and Paris on her way home.

During her absence, Watson and Crick entertained a visit from Erwin Chargaff, the scientist who had broken down the chemical nature of DNA. He was more than a bit shocked to learn of Crick's lack of understanding of the base pairs in DNA, and after listening to the two ramble on about their unsupported hypothesis for DNA's structure, Chargaff was appalled. He described Watson and Crick as "two pitchmen in search of a helix" insinuating they were trying to sell their unproven theories.

While Watson and Crick were making somewhat incautious scientific leaps, Rosalind's intellectual process was more disciplined. And while that discipline led to Photo 51, it was also a check on Rosalind's career advancement, given that the men in this race had no compunction to the same kind of discipline.

By the beginning of July, the Turner and Newall Fellowship Committee that granted Rosalind's research scholarship had contacted Randall to say that Rosalind Franklin would be performing her third year of research at Birkbeck rather than

King's. The committee letter explained that she wished to apply her X-ray crystallography knowledge to the tobacco mosaic virus (TMV) at Birkbeck. It is unclear whether Bernal and the committee had saved her the trouble of asking Randall, or whether it was simply a formality. Regardless, Randall's reaction was unmistakable. It would be easier for everyone if Rosalind left King's.

James Watson

Much later, Randall said he'd been glad to transfer her fellowship to Birkbeck. Whether she had made arrangements at Birkbeck or whether he first suggested to her that it would be better if she went elsewhere, he couldn't recall. But, speaking about his own response to Rosalind remaining at King's, he said, "The situation [at King's] was impossible." He was tired of standing between Rosalind and Wilkins, trying to keep the peace while also moving science forward.

Rosalind would soon be free of that circle of scientists, from Wilkins and Seeds to Watson and Crick, stabbing at answers and demeaning her personally. But first, she needed to wrap up her research work and leave Gosling at a good stopping point as he would rely on their collective work to write his doctoral thesis. Randall recommended that she leave on January 1, 1953, but this arrangement was kept quiet, even from Gosling.

In the middle of July 1952, Rosalind and Gosling took new readings of intensities from the dry crystalline A form. They noticed that the reflections on one side of the X axis, the horizontal line of their graph, were different from the reflections on the flip side of the X axis. As a result, Rosalind could not declare the A form a helix. With a helical structure, the intensities should be the same on each side. But the symmetry was not there. The DNA molecule, in the A form, was "lopsided." The configuration of their Signer sample's A-DNA form remained unsolved.

In late July, Rosalind crafted a prank obituary for the helical crystalline structure of A-DNA. Perhaps she was blowing off steam from her latest disappointment, or maybe she was feeling the freedom of her upcoming departure from King's, but she meant the obituary to be facetious. She sent an invitation to a pretend memorial service exclusively to Stokes and Wilkins.

It was a chaotic week at King's. The hole in the quad had finally been fixed and filled in and new lab buildings constructed. With background noises of the Physics and Engineering Departments moving their labs, Rosalind asked Gosling to gather Wilkins and Stokes and bring them to Randall's old room, which he had vacated to move into his remodeled office in an existing building.

When Wilkins and Stokes entered the room, Rosalind presented her Patterson results. Her serious tone gave the impression of an official colloquium-type gathering. Wilkins, always the nervous type, half listened while Rosalind presented the "death of the helix."

Rosalind shared how her recent work with Gosling using the Patterson method showed an asymmetrical structure and no discernable helical (or any other) pattern. The memorial card, the size of a small index card, had a thin black border that made it look like official stationery. She read the card aloud to the assembled scientists jokingly announcing the death of the helical structure of DNA.

Wilkins took Rosalind's report seriously. He wasn't paying close attention, thinking that Rosalind believed that both the

IT IS WITH GREAT REGRET THAT WE HAVE TO ANNOUNCE THE DEATH, ON FRIDAY 18TH JULY 1952 OF D.N.A. HELIX (CRYSTALLINE)

DEATH FOLLOWED A PROTRACTED ILLNESS WHICH AN INTENSIVE COURSE OF BESSELISED INJECTIONS HAD FAILED TO RELIEVE.

A MEMORIAL SERVICE WILL BE HELD NEXT MONDAY OR TUESDAY.

IT IS HOPED THAT DR. M.H.F. WILKINS WILL SPEAK IN MEMORY OF THE LATE HELIX

R. E. Franklin   R G Gosling

Rosalind's satirical note announcing the death of the DNA helix

A- and B-DNA forms were not helical even though the death announcement was only for the crystalline A form and not the paracrystalline B form. Rosalind knew the B hydrated form was a repeating pattern based on Photo 51. She had started her detailed Patterson analysis on the harder of the two forms. It would have been easier if she had chosen to work on the B form first, but by presenting her A form results in this manner, Wilkins completely misunderstood.

After the presentation was over, Wilkins asked Stokes what he thought of Rosalind's data. Stokes confirmed that, at first glance, the image of the A form she analyzed via the Patterson method seemed to indicate that its structure was not a helix.

Shortly after Rosalind's memorial service, everyone at King's lab had to prepare status reports for their funding organization, the MRC. Wilkins was leaving soon for a trip to Brazil and was in a hurry to finish his report. He wrote that "recent indications seemed not to point towards helices." This statement led Watson and Crick at Cavendish to think King's had given up on helices.

Gosling said, "Often overlooked is the fact that [Rosalind's] note was referring to the crystalline, or A form, of DNA—which after months of Patterson analysis still gave off too many artifactual X-ray diffraction patterns to allow her to rule a helical structure in or out of contention. At no time did she think the B form was anything but helical."

Why would Wilkins put this statement in his report without asking whether either form showed a helical pattern? He later explained that he'd been rushed and assumed Rosalind was indicating both were asymmetrical. This was the type of inattentive approach on Wilkins's part to interpreting Rosalind's work that made her want to leave King's and move to Birkbeck. And Wilkins's misunderstanding may later have cost Rosalind full recognition of her work and findings.

CHAPTER 10

Summer Vacations or Summer Networking

The phrase "war with women" was like "down with science" at the end of a letter to Francis Crick; it did not have the literal meaning of what I wrote. Writing in such wild ways was not very sensible and I doubt if those parts of my letter helped poor Randall. I expect he was still apologizing for now having condemned sexist rubbish.

—MAURICE WILKINS

July 1952, King's College Biophysics Lab

Most everyone in the science community had taken off for summer vacations, except for Rosalind at King's, who was focused on completing her DNA research. She reflected on her decision to apply the Patterson method first to the A-DNA form. She'd learned much from the exercise, but had she chosen to work

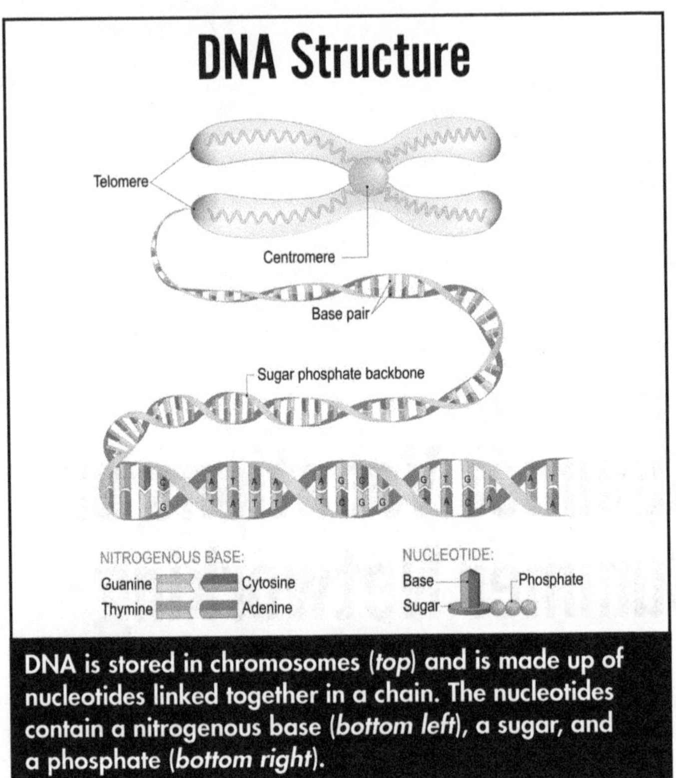

DNA is stored in chromosomes (*top*) and is made up of nucleotides linked together in a chain. The nucleotides contain a nitrogenous base (*bottom left*), a sugar, and a phosphate (*bottom right*).

on B-DNA first, she would be further along in assessing DNA structure. If she'd analyzed the B form first, she might have resolved the question of DNA structure before anyone else. And that meant she might have been able to leave King's sooner.

Her notebooks from the latter part of 1952 were filled with notes on her observations of the B form, and she wrote of it: "indication of a helix."

Analyzing the B-DNA form produced a pattern with discernable diffraction scatters that was similar to the images of coal and graphite that Rosalind had made in Paris—"sharper, but very complex." The B-DNA form was longer than A-DNA, making it easier to understand. In her notes, she detailed how the extra hydration used in her B-DNA test allowed the crystallography image to capture the lowest energy of the molecule, meaning the molecule was almost static, and that allowed for better structural images.

These new findings allowed Rosalind to calculate DNA's density, size, and water content. She now could propose a more comprehensive picture of DNA, including its structure as a double helix. And she confirmed her prior suggestion that sugar phosphates formed the external backbone of the structure. She documented the exact hydration percentages used and verified that the A-DNA form had antiparallel chains, where the sugars are parallel, but the sugars of each strand are oriented in opposite directions. She made slow progress but wanted all the necessary proof before announcing her results.

After writing his (haphazardly drafted) MRC status report, Wilkins took a long working vacation to Brazil and Peru. His mood was gloomier than usual as he'd just broken up with his girlfriend. Traveling alone with his beloved compact microscope, he also made a stop in France to speak at the International Congress of Biochemistry and to attend the Bacteriophage Conference, to be held at the Royaumont Abbey north of Paris. Wilkins later wrote, "Phage genetics have the advantage that experiments are rather fast" compared to DNA experiments. Studying bacteriophage, viruses that could infect bacteria, could potentially generate the next big breakthrough in genetics.

Since Watson had been prohibited from studying DNA, he turned his attention back to his previous research on tobacco mosaic virus. Watson also traveled to the Royaumont Abbey and was preparing to deliver a lecture for the Bacteriophage Conference. Crick was concerned that Watson might focus more on the significance of tobacco mosaic virus than DNA. And he wasn't wrong. Once Watson returned to Cavendish, Crick planned to rein his colleague back into the DNA fold, even though they were banned from pursuing the subject. Crick was hoping to finish his thesis by the end of summer and therefore be free to research DNA despite Bragg's ban.

It was late July when chemists, physicists, biologists, and physicians—with the notable exception of Rosalind Franklin—gathered at Royaumont Abbey to network and share their wisdom about bacteria. The American Phage Group were the world leaders in bacteriophage research, and that team included Max Delbrück from Caltech, Salvador Luria from the University of Illinois, and Alfred Hershey from the Carnegie Institute of Washington.

One other American researcher, Linus Pauling from Caltech, was hell-bent on attending the French conference. Considered the world's greatest chemist at the time, Pauling had professed a belief in the helical structure of DNA, but like Watson and Crick, thought it was a triple, not a double, structure. But Pauling had been stalled in the United States with passport issues in fall of 1951, when he'd been invited to speak to the Royal Society in London the following May 1952.

Pauling stood out among his scientific colleagues, and not only for his brilliant mind. He wore baggy khaki pants held up by colorful suspenders, open-toed sandals, and jaunty berets that covered his long white hair. His wife, Ava Helen Pauling, had introduced him to so-called radical ideas of socialism, pacifism, and political activism. The couple's activism during the McCarthy era when suspected "Communists" were threatened with career-ending investigations caused Pauling a lot of trouble. On Valentine's Day 1952, Pauling received his first of many passport rejection letters. Pauling wrote to President Harry

Truman asking for assistance. He attached a copy of the Medal of Merit that the president had awarded to him. But Truman wanted no part in telling the passport agency how to do their work. So, Pauling did not make it to the Royal Society meeting that May.

Pauling's travel woes likely denied one of the world's leading scientists access to Rosalind and her data. If he had been able to travel to London, spent time at King's, met and discussed DNA with Rosalind, and seen Photo 51, Pauling might well have been the first to deduce the double helical structure of DNA. Instead, his colleague Robert Corey delivered Pauling's address, and his dispassionate reading was not well received. Corey met with Rosalind at King's, and she showed him her photographs, which he admired. The two hit it off, but Corey was not the scientist that Pauling was and failed to understand the implication of Rosalind's findings and of Photo 51.

But by summer 1952, Pauling's passport problems were rapidly gaining publicity in England. His appeal went to the highest levels at the State Department. Albert Einstein himself wrote to US Secretary of State Dean Acheson. Acheson brought the issue to the press to stir up visibility and support. On July 14, just before the Royaumont conference, Pauling was finally granted his passport when he signed an affidavit attesting that he was not a Communist.

Pauling and his wife were off to Royaumont Abbey to join the event. Alfred Hershey's keynote quickly had everyone energized, including Pauling. Hershey, a gangly bespectacled geneticist, was the editor of the well-respected reference book, *Bacteriophage*. His keynote highlighted his work with lab assistant Martha Chase on experiments in the Department of Genetics at the Carnegie Institute of Washington (now the Cold Spring Harbor Laboratory of Quantitative Biology), during 1951 and 1952. What Hershey and Chase brought to the conference was invaluable. They addressed a central question about genes: Is the key molecule in genetic material a protein, or is it DNA? If Hershey and Chase could demystify the composition of phage, they would find the answer.

They started with one basic fact: Whenever bacteriophage infects bacteria, the bacteriophage replicates itself inside the cell. They developed a mechanism to tag both the DNA

Linus Pauling

Linus Pauling is the only individual winner of two Nobel Prizes. The first was a Nobel Prize in Chemistry for his work on chemical bonds. The second, the Nobel Peace Prize, was for his public disapproval of weapons of mass destruction after the United States dropped atomic bombs on the Japanese cities of Hiroshima and Nagasaki in World War II. Pauling spoke out against nuclear testing whenever he could, and he credited his wife for the Peace Prize. When the prize committee called him, he handed the telephone over to her.

In 1939 Pauling wrote the de facto book on chemistry, *The Nature of the Chemical Bond and the Structure of Molecules and Crystals*. He published over a thousand papers. His list of accolades is long, and he is considered one of the founding fathers of molecular chemistry.

But Pauling's scientific work was hampered by accusations about his left-leaning personal beliefs. In post-World-War-II America, concerns that the Communist ideologies of the rising Union of Soviet Socialist Republics (USSR or Soviet Union) were gaining traction among United States citizens prompted and the protein of bacterial viruses with distinct radioactive labels. They coated one set of bacteriophages with one type of radioactive protein and another set of bacteriophages with radioactive DNA. They infected the bacteria, and after their samples replicated, they spun the samples in the best centrifuge they had—a Waring kitchen blender—to detach the bacteriophage from the cells. After separating the phage from the cells, they traced the radioactivity in the protein and the DNA.

Linus Pauling

what became known as the "Red Scare" (red being the color associated with the Soviet Union). Conservative US Senator Joseph McCarthy ran the House Un-American Activities Committee, whose goals were to root out, expose, and prosecute Americans who espoused communism in any form. Many public figures were accused of being active Communists or of promoting Communist ideologies and were blacklisted, lost jobs, or were persecuted by McCarthy and the others in power, including FBI Director J. Edgar Hoover. Pauling was one of the thousands of public figures, government employees, private citizens, and actors harassed for their beliefs during the McCarthy era.

The radioactive protein did not replicate. But the radioactive DNA did. So, DNA directed the cellular replication.

Hershey shared these results at the conference, and the research became known as the Waring Blender experiment. Hearing Hershey's lecture, Linus Pauling's pulse raced with excitement. The result of this experiment convinced Pauling that by researching protein, he had been chasing the wrong molecule. Pauling literally sang while running from hall to hall in the abbey: "The genetic master molecule, the one that directed the making of proteins, was DNA." He understood the chemistry. Now he was certain he'd be the first to solve DNA's structure.

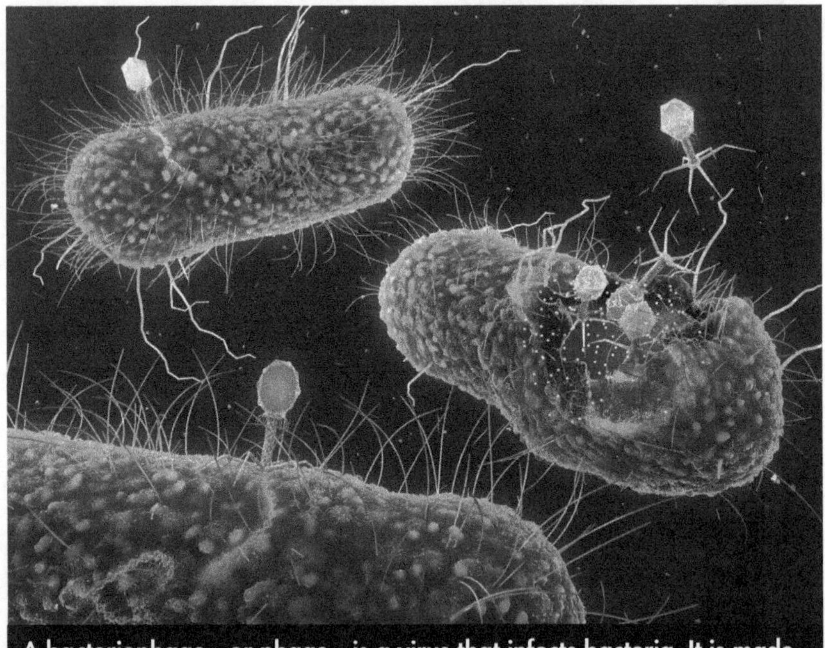

A bacteriophage—or phage—is a virus that infects bacteria. It is made of protein and nucleic acid. The phage attaches itself to a bacteria cell and inserts its genetic material. The phage rapidly replicates and kills the host bacteria cell. As many as two hundred new bacteriophages are ready to infect other bacteria.

Pauling knew that the community studying DNA structure was small. He'd heard that Rosalind and Wilkins were on the hunt for answers but assumed they wouldn't make headway because of the widely rumored infighting at King's. Plus, Pauling didn't think there was any "indication that either of them knew enough chemistry to be a serious threat." Had Pauling met with Rosalind that past May, he might have felt differently. Pauling also knew that Watson and Crick had tried to solve the DNA problem, but their failed model was legendary, and Pauling considered them not to be up to the job. Pauling believed in himself, his abilities, and his developing theory of DNA structure, and what he learned at Royaumont only confirmed this belief.

Despite Pauling's low opinion of the Cavendish crowd, his second child, Peter, was planning to enter Cambridge University. Peter would be a research student in the fall of 1952, beginning his PhD program in physics at the Cavendish lab and working with Crick and Watson. But Ava Pauling knew about Peter's excessive partying and was worried that he was entering a competitive field where his father was well known. During the conference, at a casual meeting, Ava Pauling expressed her concerns to Watson, hoping she could persuade him to keep an eye on her boy.

Watson was well aware of the power he could hold if he had Peter on his side. Peter would be able to tell Watson things about his father's research into DNA. Watson reassured her that Peter would be well looked after. Indeed, once Peter arrived at Cavendish, he and Watson became fast friends, and this friendship helped to tip the DNA race in Cavendish's favor.

After Royaumont, Watson took time off. He hiked around the Italian Alps and afterward attended a microbial genetics meeting. There he became obsessed with the research of twenty-two-year-old Joshua Lederberg of the University of Wisconsin. Or more accurately Watson was obsessed with Lederberg's meteoric rise as the new scientific "wunderkind" and his research on bacteria and genetic recombination. Watson sent a letter to Crick mentioning Lederberg's work, which only reinforced Crick's concern that Watson would no longer be interested in DNA. Crick had finally finished his thesis and was hoping to get back into the DNA race.

Wilkins had learned that Rosalind was leaving King's, and he decided not to think about DNA until she was gone. He didn't think it was worth it to be in a rush, as Crick did. Wilkins was only happy to be away from his ongoing war with Rosalind and to know that she was leaving King's. While still in Europe, Wilkins had written to Crick, "Franklin barks often

A Paper or a Letter?

Professional journals such as *Nature* require that scientific papers submitted for publication go through peer review. Scientists of equal caliber read the papers and establish that the science follows standard methods of analysis, whether or not the conclusions are correct.

Letters are informal and not required to undergo peer review. They also do not have the credibility of a peer-reviewed paper.

but doesn't succeed in biting me. Since I reorganized my time so that I can concentrate on the job, she no longer gets under my skin. I was in a bad way about it all when I last saw you." His trip to South America following the conference at Royaumont was a respite.

Back in London, Rosalind was hard at work, finishing up. Her lab notebooks from 1952 up to her departure from King's show that she considered the B-DNA form helical. She translated her results into a paper for the journal *Nature*, titled "Evidence for a 2-Chain Helix in the Crystalline Structure of Sodium Deoxyribonucleate." But her disdain for the kind of scientific competition exhibited by the men around her showed in the slow pace of her work and her focus on exiting the toxic environment at King's.

After the Royaumont conference, Pauling, believing that he held a key to DNA's structure and convinced of DNA's role as the secret to the origin of life, headed to Cavendish to discuss protein helical structures with Crick. He was entering the DNA space that Rosalind was preparing to leave. And Pauling considered the search for the answer to DNA's structure to be not only a competition but a race.

CHAPTER 11

Pauling and Pauling

Everyone who touched DNA seemed to go a little crazy. . . . DNA was like the gold of Midas—touch it and you go mad.

—MAURICE WILKINS

August 1952, Cavendish College

After the Royaumont conference, Pauling headed to Cavendish. He wanted Bragg, the head of Cavendish, to introduce him to Francis Crick. Earlier that year, Crick had sent Pauling an advanced copy of a research paper to be published that September, and authored by Crick and two other Cavendish colleagues, William Cochran and Vladimir Vand, titled "The Structure of Synthetic Polypeptides. I. The Transform of Atoms on a Helix."

The second section of the paper really caught Pauling's eye because it discussed the "Fourier transforms of identical atoms spaced at regular intervals on a helix." Pauling had known that the protein α-Keratin was helical, but he didn't yet understand the mathematical formula for predicting how helixes would diffract X-rays, a key to discerning DNA structure. He was hoping that Crick would enlighten him.

This was ironic. Pauling's own studies on proteins had prompted Cavendish to study the correlations between helixes and diffraction of X-rays. When Bragg took Crick and Watson off everything DNA, Bragg steered Crick toward the alternate assignment of demystifying the diffraction patterns that bounced off a helix. Crick had been incredibly pleased about finding the formula. He'd sent Pauling a preprint of his paper because he was showcasing his first significant scientific success. For Crick, Pauling's visit to Cambridge after Royaumont became an exercise in establishing his own bona fides.

Pauling was nothing if not clever. Crick was starstruck by the man who had done monumental work on protein structures. Pauling was then fifty-two years old, and Crick, thirty-six. During lunch at a Cambridge pub, Pauling invited Crick to come work with him at Caltech for a year. Disarmed and charmed, Crick openly shared a new theory on alpha helixes. Crick asked Pauling, "Ever considered whether or not the alpha helixes might be coiled around one another?"

Crick called this form of alpha helixes "coiled coils." Pauling said he had considered it, when in fact the extent of his knowledge is not clear. Instead, Pauling pretended to be indifferent on the subject.

While in England, Pauling also met with other scientists at Cavendish including Bragg and Perutz, but he didn't visit King's or meet with Rosalind or Wilkins, who surely would have discussed their DNA research with him. Pauling remained ignorant of Rosalind's extraordinary images, especially Photo 51. He left England and went back to Caltech to work on his protein problem. Crick's suggestion that so-called coiled coil structures could be twisted around each other was at the top of his mind. Pauling told his colleagues, "This [coiled coil] form could provide the missing X-ray reflection that the alpha helix alone did not."

After they parted, Crick became worried that he'd shared his theory on helix structure too openly with Pauling. What if Crick had led Pauling to the information that would complete Pauling's own explanation of the protein alpha-helix? The helical structures Crick observed in proteins could even provide Pauling with the answer to the DNA structure question. As Crick observed, "Helices were in the air, and you would have to be either obtuse or very obstinate not to think along helical lines."

Rightly afraid Pauling would beat him to publication with his own information, Crick took precautionary measures. He wrote a "Letter to the Editor" of *Nature* to let the publication know of his coiled coil premise and titled it "Is α-Keratin a Coiled Coil?"

Pauling was obsessed with finishing his research on protein structures, and with Crick's unwitting collaboration, he finished it. Pauling sent *Nature* a full article on alpha-keratin. He coauthored it with Robert Corey, and their paper discussed how alpha-keratin protein could twist about itself, forming "coiled coils." They called their paper, "Compound Helical Configurations of Polypeptide Chains: Structures of Proteins of the α-Keratin Type."

Pauling's article to *Nature* was received before Crick's letter. But, because articles go through a vetting process and "Letters" do not, Crick's letter was published first, on November 22, 1952, with Pauling's article appearing on January 10, 1953.

In September 1952, Wilkins returned home from Brazil. He looked around his Soho apartment filled with items that reminded him of Edel, his ex-girlfriend. He said, "I exploded: for a moment out of character, I smashed the beautiful things Edel had given me over the years." After this emotional outburst, he decided to put Edel behind him, and he replaced the losses with new things he had bought on his South American trip.

Wilkins's mood was lifted at the publication of an article he'd written at Randall's suggestion for *Nature* on the advances in spectroscopy made by the Biophysics Department at King's. But it wasn't at all cheerful for Wilkins at the lab. He told visiting scientist Herbert Wilson not to bother asking Rosalind for any of the Signer DNA samples. Wilkins later recalled telling Wilson, "Rosalind seemed so negative that I did not want to be involved in asking her for anything," adding, "I decided to 'Go back to my microscopes' until Rosalind had got further on with her non-helical DNA."

By mid-September, Watson also was home from his travels. Before he got back to business at Cavendish, he checked on what was happening at other labs. He asked about King's model building. It had been almost half a year since he and Crick had reluctantly sent Rosalind the materials after their DNA model debacle. Wilkins shared with Watson and Crick that things were still difficult at King's and that they weren't using the materials, and he asked if they might want the materials back. Noting the tense King's atmosphere, Watson observed later, "Rather than build helical models at Maurice's command, she [Rosalind] might twist the copper-wire models about his neck."

Watson had made progress with tobacco mosaic virus (TMV) at Cavendish. A new anode X-ray tube doubled his

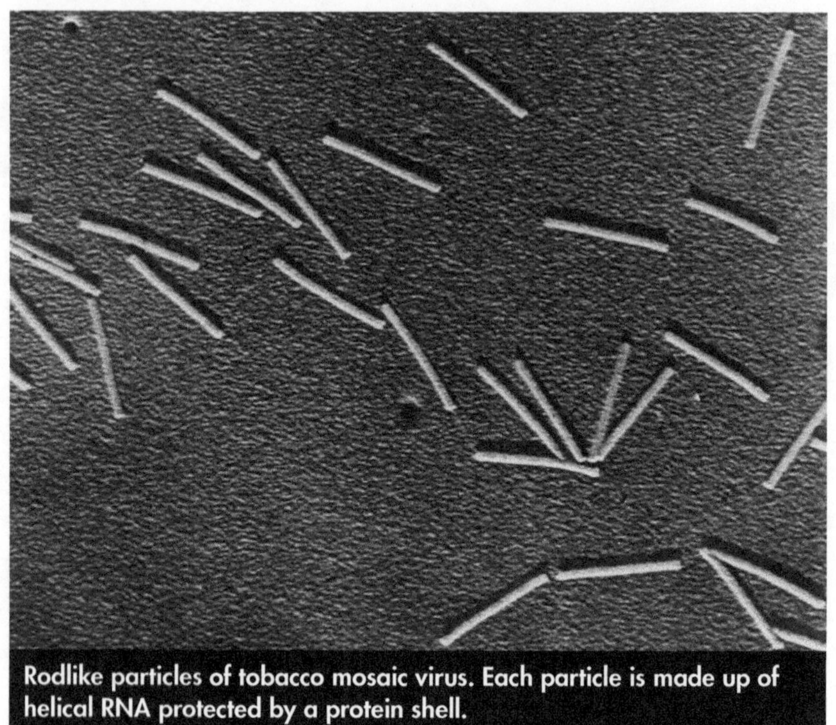

Rodlike particles of tobacco mosaic virus. Each particle is made up of helical RNA protected by a protein shell.

capacity to create the TMV images. He said, "The fact that I was doing serious X-ray work with TMV gave [Wilkins] assurance that I should not soon again become preoccupied with the DNA pattern." But Watson was done with TMV, and he was still preoccupied with DNA, declaring, "No more dividends could come quickly from TMV. Further unraveling of its detailed structure needed a more professional attack than I could muster. The way to DNA was not through TMV."

Crick no longer needed to worry about his collaborator's priorities. Watson had come back to DNA.

In November 1952, Rosalind told Gosling that she would be leaving for Birkbeck. He couldn't blame her. Gosling saw firsthand how she had been treated at King's, although he'd been blind to the depth of animosity between her and Wilkins.

But he didn't like the thought of completing his thesis without Rosalind—his adviser—by his side. He appreciated her combative style. He said she had taught him "the value of being a devil's advocate," and how to professionally defend his ideas. It would be that much more challenging for Gosling to finish his thesis under the supervision of Randall and Wilkins, especially given that Randall told Gosling that he didn't want to review Gosling's thesis until it was submitted. And Wilkins wasn't as accessible as Rosalind. Gosling did finish his thesis on his X-ray studies of DNA, but only because Rosalind helped him on the sly after she left King's.

After finishing his protein work during fall 1952, Pauling was restless, and he turned his attention toward DNA. He said, "I always thought that sooner or later I would find the structure of DNA, it was just a matter of time."

Pauling poured over Astbury's 1938 images and scoured any paper he could get his hands on regarding nucleic acid chemistry. He listened to lectures and looked at related publications in all the journals. While he had no actual data with sizes, diffraction info, or angles, and certainly nothing like the images Rosalind and Gosling had produced, he sat at his desk with a pencil, a sheaf of paper, and a slide rule. Pauling did calculations knowing that Astbury's images showed reflections. After five lines of calculations, Pauling wrote, "Perhaps we have a triple-chain structure!"

Pauling based all his subsequent conclusions on the belief that DNA had a triple, rather than double, helix structure. He wrote that it was "a question of phosphate structural chemistry. If the structure was right, the biological importance would fall out of it naturally in some way." Pauling made it his mission to fit the phosphates into the core of three helixes. His assumption mirrored what Watson and Crick had built into their incorrect model—the model that Rosalind had annihilated—by placing the phosphate groups inside the helix. Pauling was not concerned about Rosalind's response to the inaccurate Watson/Crick model. He was still ignorant of what her own images suggested.

"We have, we believe, discovered the structure of nucleic acids," Linus Pauling told Alex Todd at Cambridge and Jerry Donohue at Caltech. "I have practically no doubt. The structure really is a beautiful one." Ignoring the drawbacks of, first, packing the triple helix molecule too tightly by jamming the base pairs inside, and second, of having to explain cell replication, Pauling built his own model.

Pauling considered himself in a race with only the Cavendish team. By this time, Linus's son Peter was a student at Cavendish and close friends with Watson. Perhaps it was Linus Pauling's hubris, or maybe his wish to taunt the Brits, but he knew Peter was a two-way informant operating across the pond, from his father in California to Watson and Crick in the United Kingdom and back. Linus wrote to his son letting Peter know that he would soon produce a paper with colleague Robert Corey on DNA, and Peter shared this information with Watson.

Feeling triumphant, Pauling then pulled a Watson and Crick. He invited people to see his "extraordinarily tightly-packed model" of DNA. It was December 25, 1952, and he wanted accolades from his colleagues and staff. Pauling then wrote to Randall at King's and told him that he had found the structure of DNA, and he had submitted his paper for publication in the *Proceedings of the National Academy of Sciences*, or *PNAS*.

Dear Randall:

I have never seen the photographs made in your laboratory, but I understand that they are much better than those of Astbury and Bell, whereas ours are inferior to Astbury and Bell's. We are hoping to obtain better photographs, but fortunately the photographs we have are good enough to permit the derivation of our structure.

Sincerely yours,
Linus Pauling

Pauling's article was a rush job, to be published in *PNAS* on February 1, 1953, and titled "A Proposed Structure for the Nucleic Acids."

On December 31, in what was seen as preempting everyone else's research, Pauling also submitted two paragraphs announcing their DNA structure in a letter to *Nature* to publish February 21, 1953. It read, "We have formulated a structure for the nucleic acids which is compatible with the main features of the X-ray diagram and with the general principles of molecular structure, and which accounts satisfactorily for some of the chemical properties of the substances. The structure involves three intertwined helical polynucleotide chains." Pauling referred in the last paragraph to their forthcoming article. Linus Pauling and his proposed triple helix DNA structure were about to be everywhere.

CHAPTER 12

Caught Red-Handed

I explained how I was racing Peter's father for the Nobel Prize.

—JAMES WATSON

December 1952–January 1953, King's College Biophysics Lab and Cavendish College

The Cavendish crowd got wind of Linus Pauling's accomplishment in December 1952. Watson believed that the English were about to be humiliated by the Americans and left for a skiing holiday in Switzerland. On the way home from his ski holiday, Watson stopped by King's to let Wilkins know about Pauling's proclamation. He countered Watson's news with his own, that Rosalind would soon be gone, saying, "I had recently been relieved to hear that Rosalind was going to leave our lab for a post at Birkbeck College."

At King's, Rosalind was absent at the end of term, due to a bout with flu, which accounted in part for her initial silence on the Pauling revelation. She had planned to leave King's by the first of January, but her departure was delayed by two months primarily because she wanted to finish all her remaining work, and she'd lost time with the flu. She was busy proofing two papers, already accepted for publication, and polishing a third paper with Gosling establishing their finding on the helical structure of the B form of DNA.

A final presentation summarizing Rosalind's research at King's was widely anticipated, and Wilkins's fixation about it was unmistakable. He told Crick when the lecture would take place, and added, "Let's have some talks afterwards when the air is a little clearer. I hope the smoke of witchcraft will soon be getting out of our eyes."

By January 1, 1953, Rosalind had got wind of Pauling and Corey's DNA breakthrough. On January 6, she wrote Corey asking for details, having become friendly with him since he had praised her photographs that past year. Her curiosity about the Pauling-Corey findings is clear from writings in her January notebooks. For perhaps the first time, she thought about building a model based on her Patterson method findings. She was sure that the B-DNA form was a double helix but still had doubts about the A form. She mused about Erwin Chargaff's well-documented ratios of the proteins but couldn't place them structurally in a way that would also work chemically. And she was running up against the deadline for her move to Birkbeck.

In mid-to-late January, Gosling approached Wilkins in the hallway of the lab at King's, bearing Photo 51. Wilkins recalled, "Raymond [Gosling] met me in the corridor and handed me an excellent B pattern that Rosalind and he had taken. For me to be shown raw data in such a way was quite without precedent and, even more extraordinary, Raymond made it clear that I was to keep the photograph!"

Wilkins knew the photo represented a helical structure of the B form "more clearly than ever before." He was impressed—and not just with Gosling's gesture, given the state of things between Wilkins and Rosalind. He understood what the photograph, taken almost nine months earlier, meant. It was concrete proof that the structure of the B form was a double, and not a triple, helix. This meant that Pauling was wrong.

Neither Wilkins nor Gosling was clear later on the details of this hallway transaction, and both repeatedly contradicted their own memories. Rosalind never mentioned anything about it. Did she give Photo 51 to Gosling with the understanding that he would then give it to Wilkins, a man she could barely tolerate? And why didn't Wilkins approach Rosalind with the photograph, and discuss its implication with her? Whatever the answers to these questions, it led to a haunting loss for Rosalind.

On January 28, Rosalind gave her final seminar at King's, summarizing her two years of work there. Wilkins was in the audience. He waited to hear her use the word *helix*, but she didn't. His initial takeaway was that Rosalind talked "exceptionally long, and solely about her structure for A-DNA."

Rosalind presented the analyses she'd completed with Gosling that "suggested that the A form of the molecule was not helical."

She also presented a structural model that Wilkins described as "bent pieces of wire, zigzags, and figure-of-eight shapes." At the end of her presentation, Wilkins, having now seen Photo 51, questioned why she hadn't brought up the helical B-DNA form. Rosalind shot back that the B-DNA was helical, so that was a nonissue. Her concern had been researching the obscure A-DNA form and determining its structure, and she believed that was where the real challenge and answers are. Rosalind repeated what she had told him the day she made the memorial card for the A-DNA crystalline form: There was not yet a case to call A-DNA helical.

Rosalind's conclusions at the time about the structure of both forms were clearly stated in her lab notebooks and other presentations. But this was the first time that Wilkins paid close enough attention to understand what she'd been saying for months. Wilkins was stunned. He said, "I was taken aback by her answer, because that was the first time I heard her concede that any DNA could be helical. I was even more surprised that she thought B-DNA was helical and A-DNA was not. I do not think it had ever occurred to me that she might believe that."

Wilkins later wrote, "Why did she not show it [Photo 51]?" The other question is, Why did Wilkins not refer directly to the photograph and ask her about it during her presentation or afterward? The answer to the latter may be because she didn't know that he had the photograph, and perhaps his reluctance to mention it implies some guilt on his part.

Wilkins did the only thing he could: He planned a social weekend with Crick to vent. Wilkins told Crick that he needed some cheering up. He said, "Rosie's colloquium made me a bit sicker. God knows what will become of all this business." Wilkins felt that Rosalind's conclusions were confusing. How could the B-DNA form be helical, but the A-DNA form be something else? He added, "Her lack of faith in intuition is in line with her wanting to base conclusions solely on hard facts which spoke for themselves. Science can never be as simple as that."

Lawrence Bragg

Linus Pauling informed his son Peter that he was sending a preprint of the *PNAS* paper to Bragg and asked if Peter would also care to see it. Peter told his father to please send it along. The preprint of the paper arrived in both Bragg's and Peter's mailboxes at Cavendish on January 28, the same day as Rosalind's final presentation. Bragg ignored Pauling's paper when it arrived, but Peter brought the preprint into Watson's office, where Crick was also present.

Watson listened impatiently as Peter tried to summarize its contents, the paper itself sticking out of Peter's jacket pocket. Watson finally yanked the paper away from Peter and read it. He knew within a few paragraphs that Linus had made the same mistake in the structure that he and Crick had made by putting the phosphate pairs on the inside of the molecule. Further, Pauling, believing firmly in his model, had made a basic error in chemistry. That raised Watson's and Crick's hopes. But because the paper had been accepted for publication, that error once revealed to the world would make Pauling more desperate to uncover the true structure.

Crick had nearly been usurped to publication with Pauling's reference to Crick's coiled coils. That wound was still fresh. The Cavendish group didn't want the Americans to take the DNA prize. The Cavendish team—including administrator John Kendrew, Max Perutz (director of Cambridge's Medical Research Council Biophysics Unit), Watson, and Crick—understood the stakes. Watson and Crick confronted Kendrew and Perutz with Pauling's preprint, and the two administrators immediately lifted the moratorium against the two scientists' pursuit of DNA structure. Watson and Crick had until the Pauling and Corey paper appeared in the *PNAS* about six weeks later to come to their solution.

Watson and Crick's only concern was what Bragg and Randall would have to say about Kendrew and Perutz's action. Especially Randall, in light of his having given Rosalind full rein on the DNA problem. Crick said in a later interview, "They were mucking about at King's, getting nowhere. Don't you see, if I hadn't done something about it, Pauling would have got it out first. Oh, I know Linus was wrong with his first guess, but Linus isn't stupid like Maurice—he'd have done it." Despite Crick's insinuation about Wilkins's abilities, he knew that the solution to getting to the real DNA structure was to bring Wilkins—who had not focused on the Pauling breakthrough nor seen the preprint but who did have access to anything valuable at King's—on board.

Time was of the essence. And Rosalind was out of the picture.

On January 30, Watson took a train to London, carrying a copy of the preprint. He met with a colleague at Hammersmith Hospital to discuss finishing a paper and then made his way to King's. Watson found Wilkins and tried to explain the Pauling model, but Wilkins appeared disinterested. Wilkins remained uncomfortable around Watson, regardless of Watson's friendship with Crick, and had come to consider Watson (as did Randall and Bragg) something of a dilettante and a pest. Wilkins said later that the thought of

Crick and Watson "beginning the DNA Race again was so little to my liking that I managed not to think about it." After half listening to Watson's explanation and the dismantling of Pauling's DNA theory, Wilkins must have asked himself, Had Linus solved the DNA puzzle? Was there still room for study? Wilkins knew from Rosalind's Photo 51 and what she'd said at her colloquium that there was.

Rosalind was still working in the same windowless basement lab she'd been assigned to in 1951. On that particular evening of January 30, she was working right through teatime, focused on the measurements, reading them from a diffraction photo with a microscope over a light table. The room was otherwise dark so that she could better see the minute images.

Watson left Wilkins and hurried down the hallway. He likely went to Rosalind to fulfill his need for someone to listen to his opinions about the Pauling model, since as he said later, he was hoping she would be about. He didn't knock on Rosalind's lab door. He found the door ajar and barged in. Rosalind was startled and irritated at the intrusion. Her time at King's was running out, and she still had so much to finish. Earlier in the month, she'd entered the lab and surprised someone reading her notebooks. She was primed to be upset, her adrenaline no doubt running high.

Twenty-five-year-old Watson had always had trouble with women (he and Peter Pauling were well known as skirt chasers), and particularly with independent and intelligent women. He still held a grudge against Rosalind for pointing out the inaccuracies in his and Crick's November 1951 model, and he never considered her his intellectual equal. But there he was, with Pauling's preprint in hand.

Rosalind told Watson at once that he was inappropriate. Instead of apologizing, he launched into his interpretation of the Pauling-Corey findings, explaining them to her as if she was an ignorant student, and handed her the preprint. Scanning the paper further upset Rosalind. She'd thought she had a good relationship with Corey. He'd seen and praised her images when they'd met the previous May. She'd asked him for a copy of this very paper, and here it was in Watson's hands. Moreover, Pauling and Corey had based their findings on Astbury's 1938 images, and they acknowledged images taken by Wilkins in 1951, but they didn't mention Rosalind's 1952 images.

It was insulting and humiliating, and Watson was explaining science that Rosalind already knew. She lost her temper and lit into him. She knew that the B form was helical. She knew her images were the best in the world. She had evidence of DNA's true structure, and she was sure Watson didn't understand what he was looking at. He bit back and called her incompetent.

That was enough for Rosalind. She came around from behind her lab bench. As he recounted the scene, Watson, who was over 6 feet (1.8 m) tall, was frightened by the 5 foot 4 (1.6 m) slender Rosalind. He worried she would hit him. He grabbed the preprint and left. And ran straight into Wilkins, who was lurking in the doorway. The two men hesitated in surprise, and when they moved into the hall, Rosalind slammed the door in their wake.

Something snapped in Wilkins in that moment. He admitted to Watson that Rosalind had once "made a similar lunge toward him," probably referring to the incident in 1951 following the Gordon Research Conference, when Rosalind yelled at him for inserting himself into her research. Her angry outburst had startled Wilkins then, and he felt sympathy for Watson and antipathy for Rosalind. Never mind that her anger was earned in both cases.

Wilkins told Watson that Rosalind had evidence of DNA structure. Watson, surprised, asked Wilkins, "What the pattern was like."

Wilkins made what appears to have been an instantaneous decision. Watson later said, "Maurice went into the adjacent room to pick up a print of the new form they called the 'B' structure" of DNA. It was Rosalind's Photo 51. Wilkins's abrupt change of heart remains unexplained (it goes unmentioned in his autobiography, and it is only represented through Watson). But, like Rosalind's reaction to Watson, Wilkins may have reached a boiling point after the months of tension. And he must have understood the consequences of his action.

In that moment, Wilkins turned his back on Rosalind and gave away her research to Watson.

Rosalind recognized her photograph's importance but refused to reach further conclusions about DNA structure until she had analyzed the A form. Watson wasn't one to wait for anything. The instant he saw the photo he knew what he was looking at, just as Wilkins and Rosalind had. "My mouth fell open and my pulse began to race," Watson said.

After eating dinner with Wilkins, Watson boarded a frigid train for the ride home. He'd realized that Wilkins, although he understood the significance of the photo, didn't seem to have the passion for racing to the Nobel finish line. But Watson did, and he knew Crick did too. By the time Watson reached the Cambridge station, he'd sketched what he saw in Rosalind's photo in the margins of a newspaper. He was sure that this was the proof he needed to upstage Pauling on the structure of DNA. He just needed Crick to complete the math.

Rosalind was, at that moment, reaching a similar conclusion. Her notebooks from the following weeks are filled with

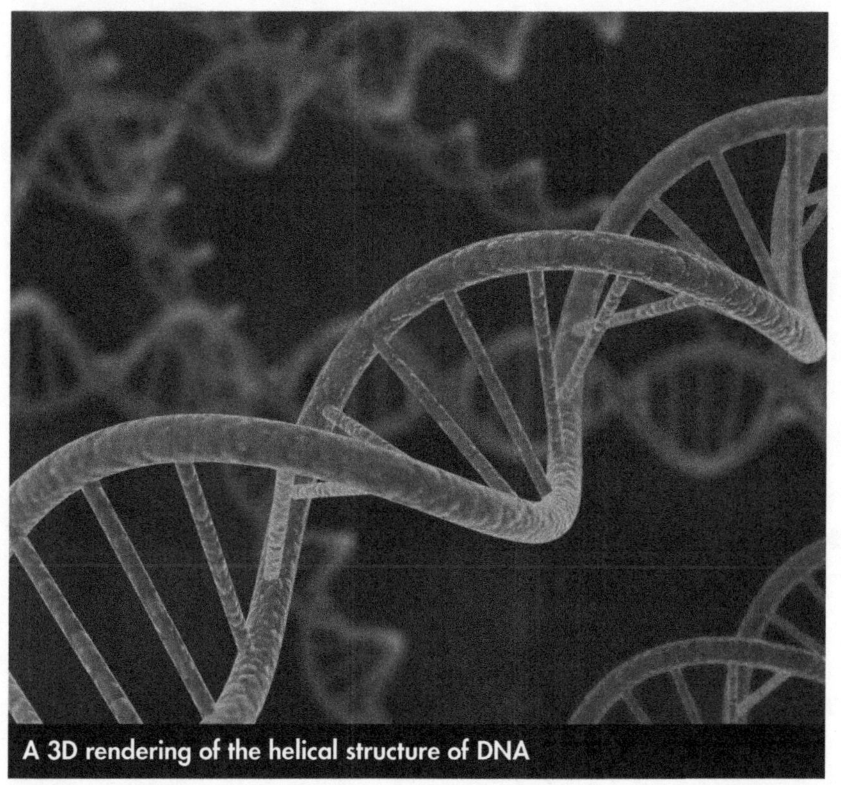
A 3D rendering of the helical structure of DNA

speculations, observations, and close calculations as to describing true DNA structure as helical. But unlike Watson, who collaborated with Crick and Wilkins, Rosalind worked alone. Once again, isolation and the lack of mentorship became Rosalind's enemy.

CHAPTER 13

Proof Is in the Pudding

Do you have any regrets, Miss Franklin. And Miss Franklin apparently said, "No, we all stand on each other's shoulders."

—RAYMOND GOSLING

February–March 1953, King's College Biophysics Lab and Cavendish College

Rosalind didn't dwell on Wilkins's reaction to her exit lecture or whether Watson and Crick were adhering to their research moratorium at Cavendish. That was no longer her problem. She focused on completing her DNA work at King's and the business of B-DNA's structure was one of her last formal interpretations for the lab.

Rosalind wanted to make certain that Chargaff's rules that the phosphates were on the outside of the DNA structure conformed with her now firm interpretation of the B-DNA structure as a double helix. She'd read and recognized the flaws in

Pauling and Corey's paper. As Watson and Crick had done in November 1951, Pauling proposed a three-helix structure with phosphates on the inside. The Pauling-Corey letter to *Nature* published on February 21 doubled down on their incorrect hypothesis.

Watson and Crick were racing to make a solid discovery and claim it as their own. At one point, Watson thought he'd cracked the structure, and without offering details he announced enough information to tease the scientific community. He said only that it "was completely different from Pauling's." But just as fast as he announced success, he realized that this first theory was "nonsense."

Sometime between February 10 and 20, 1953, another scientist betrayed Rosalind's hard work. This one remained secret to the scientific world for many years after, though known within the Cavendish community. Randall sent Max Perutz a blurry copy of the King's MRC Biophysics report that included the results of Franklin and Gosling's two years of research. Perutz then passed it on to Watson and Crick.

The consequences of this betrayal were enormous. Crick read Rosalind's paper and knew immediately what it meant. He could visualize the double-chain structure and how each of the base pairs were connected in opposition: A-C-G-T in one strand and T-G-C-A in the other strand allowing the pairs across from each other to bond as required to form the molecule. Watson and Crick ordered a metal purine and pyrimidine backbone to be constructed from their metalworking shop at Cavendish. While he was waiting for that to be finished, Watson made his own models out of cardboard. He moved the cardboard models around on his desk until "all the hydrogen bonds seemed to form naturally; no fudging was required to make the two types of base pairs identical in shape."

Francis Crick

Suddenly, as Watson fiddled with the structure, Chargaff's rules of DNA chemistry made sense. Watson said, "The hydrogen-bonding requirement meant that adenine would always pair with thymine, while guanine could pair only with cytosine."

But it was Rosalind's findings and Crick's understanding of the chemical structure that truly had solved the riddle. Adding Rosalind and Gosling's knowledge that the sugar-phosphate backbone was on the outside was vital and led to a structure of two chains of purines and pyrimidines running in different directions. Crick admitted, "We needed a clue to get to that point, and the clue was Rosalind Franklin's data."

Watson and Crick had created a double helical structure that worked with Chargaff's chemical rules, a solution that would not have been possible without Rosalind's Photo 51 and her corresponding data. It was March 1, 1953. Crick was ecstatic. Watson "subsequently admitted to feeling 'slightly queasy'" when at lunch Crick winged into the Eagle pub "telling anyone within earshot that we had found the secret of life."

Their metal models were not ready, but they couldn't present a cardboard version. Still worried that Pauling would get to the answer first, Watson visited the shop at Cavendish on March 2 and requested they speed up their production. The final soldering was accomplished in a couple of hours. Watson fiddled with the model for another fifteen minutes and then Crick inspected and approved it. The model was over 6 feet (1.8 m) tall. Crick said, "If we [he and Watson] deserve any credit at all, it is for persistence and the willingness to discard ideas when they became untenable." Crick later gave credit to Rosalind, Wilkins, and Chargaff, saying that he and Watson "guessed the correct structure, using some of the experimental data of the London group together with Chargaff's rules about the relative amounts of the four bases in different sorts of DNA."

At dinner on March 2, Watson and Crick discussed how to announce their discovery. They wanted to tell Wilkins but knew that they needed to keep King's in the dark "until exact coordinates had been obtained for all the atoms." With so much at stake, they took the next few days to make sure the atoms were in the correct positions within the nucleotide using a measuring stick and a vertical line to check that their model was plumb.

Once they'd established their model would work, neither of them wanted to make that call to King's, fearing a repeat of their November 1951 fiasco. So John Kendrew was tasked with calling Wilkins. That same day, Crick received a letter from Wilkins telling them he was turning his attention to DNA. "I intend," Wilkins wrote, "to place emphasis on model building." He once again belittled Rosalind and her contributions. He said, "Our dark lady leaves us next week and much of the 3-dimensional data is already in our hands."

On March 6, Rosalind and Gosling submitted two papers to *Acta Crystallographica*. The first focused on the water content and its influence on the structures of DNA single fibers, and the second detailed the symmetrical Patterson function of DNA. In the second paper, Rosalind stated that B pattern photographs—especially Photo 51—were "very strongly characteristic of a helical structure."

Six days later, Kendrew broke the news to Wilkins that

Watson and Crick had discovered the solution to DNA structure. When Wilkins arrived to examine their model, Crick chattered on about what an X-ray diagram should show. But Crick could tell that Wilkins wanted to see the double helix model and "not receive a lecture in crystallographic theory which he could work out by himself."

The Cavendish crew required Rosalind's and Gosling's X-rays to bring credence to their model. They needed Wilkins's cooperation. Watson said, "There was not a hint of bitterness in his [Wilkins's] voice, and I felt quite relieved. Until the visit I had remained apprehensive that he would look gloomy, being unhappy that we had seized part of the glory that should have gone in full to him and his younger colleagues. But there was no trace of resentment on his face, and in his subdued way he was thoroughly excited that the structure would prove of great benefit to biology."

But privately, Wilkins was devastated. King's had been scooped by Cavendish, and he had been partly responsible for completing Watson and Crick's theory. He'd given them Photo 51, and Randall had sent them the MRC report. After Wilkins returned to King's to reveal the news to colleagues there, Randall telephoned Bragg. The two department heads agreed that a King's paper written by Wilkins would be published simultaneously with the Cavendish paper, giving King's some credit for the discovery.

By the time Wilkins saw the model at Cavendish, Rosalind had departed for Birkbeck. It was a week later that she learned of the Cavendish success. She was setting up her new lab space when Gosling arrived to inform her of the Cavendish triumph.

She called Randall to demand that a third paper, one written by her and Gosling and already well under way about their Photo 51, be included with the others.

When she and Gosling viewed the Watson and Crick model on March 19, Rosalind agreed it was correct. She said that her X-ray data supported the double helix of the B form. She could see that Watson and Crick also made the double helix structure work for the A form and gave them credit for their success. Watson was willing to be generous. He said, "With obvious pleasure, Rosy showed Francis her data and for the first time he was able to see how foolproof was her assertion that the sugar-phosphate backbone was on the outside of the molecule." And he added, "Her past uncompromising statements on this matter thus reflected first-rate science, not the outpouring of a misguided feminist."

Watson said further, "I had feared that her sharp, stubborn mind, caught in her self-made antihelical trap might dig up irrelevant results that would foster uncertainty of the double helix," but that didn't come to fruition. Instead, he said, "Her fierce annoyance with Francis and me collapsed, . . . and [Rosalind] was prepared to exchange unconcealed hostility for conversation between equals." Rosalind was gracious in the face of the men's scientific coup, while Watson gave the King's team backhanded compliments.

Linus Pauling was still trying to create a model when word reached him of the Cavendish success. Pauling's latest attempts were still way off base. On his way to a meeting in Brussels, Pauling visited Cambridge to see Peter as well as the model. Although he liked the model at first sight, he asked to see the X-ray evidence from King's, and said, only then would he concede the race. It took him some time to conclude that the Cavendish structure was correct.

Left to right: Watson and Crick with their 1953 model of the structure of DNA

Watson and Crick loomed over Watson's sister, called in for Saturday duty to type the nine-hundred-word article titled "Molecular Structure of Nucleic Acids: A Structure for Deoxyribose Nucleic Acid." It began, "We wish to suggest a structure for the salt of deoxyribose nucleic acid (DNA). This structure has novel features which are of considerable biological interest." They sent the typed paper to Bragg's office, and on April 2, it went off to the editors of *Nature.*

Wilkins, Stokes, and Wilson's write-up was titled "Molecular Structure of Nucleic Acids: Molecular Structure of Deoxypentose Nucleic Acids" and ran second in order of publication. The Franklin and Gosling paper, "Molecular Configuration in Sodium Thymonucleate" was third in line.

All three articles appeared in that order in the April 25, 1953, edition of *Nature.* The order of publication is important in suggesting a hierarchy of discovery, with Watson and Crick taking premier credit for defining the biological/chemical structure of DNA, Wilkins's work placing second, and Rosalind and Gosling's work appearing last.

On July 8, 1953, Rosalind added this note to both of the *Acta Crystallographica* articles she coauthored with Gosling, papers that were written before Watson and Crick made their discovery: "Nevertheless, since the change A = B is readily reversible, if a two-chain helical molecule exists in structure B it must persist as such in structure A, though the dimensions of the helix may be altered." These papers were published on September 10, 1953.

Upon hearing about the discovery, Crick's wife, Odile, didn't believe they had accomplished such a thing. Odile said to her husband, "You were always coming home and saying things like that so naturally I thought nothing of it." Francis and Odile eventually named their family home The Golden Helix after the discovery, and Crick added a helix medallion to the front of the house.

Bragg didn't see the actual model immediately because he was ill with the flu. When he saw the structure all past differences were forgiven, and he became one of the strongest supporters of the theory. Randall later related to Anne Sayre that it was partly the troubles between Rosalind and Wilkins that resulted in the Cambridge triumph. Randall added that it was "only justice" that Wilkins shared in the Nobel Prize.

Watson said, "It seemed almost unbelievable that the DNA structure was solved, that the answer was incredibly exciting, and that our names would be associated with the double helix as Pauling's was with the alpha helix." One evening Watson explained the double helix's main points to scientists at Cambridge. As he finished, all he was able to say through teary eyes was, "It's so beautiful, you see, so beautiful!"

Rosalind's contribution to DNA research while she was at King's has only recently begun to receive the attention it deserves. As Aaron Klug, a researcher at Birkbeck, would later say, "What she touched, she adorned." This was true of her study of DNA, and at Birkbeck she was about to turn her touch on the study of viruses and the structure of RNA.

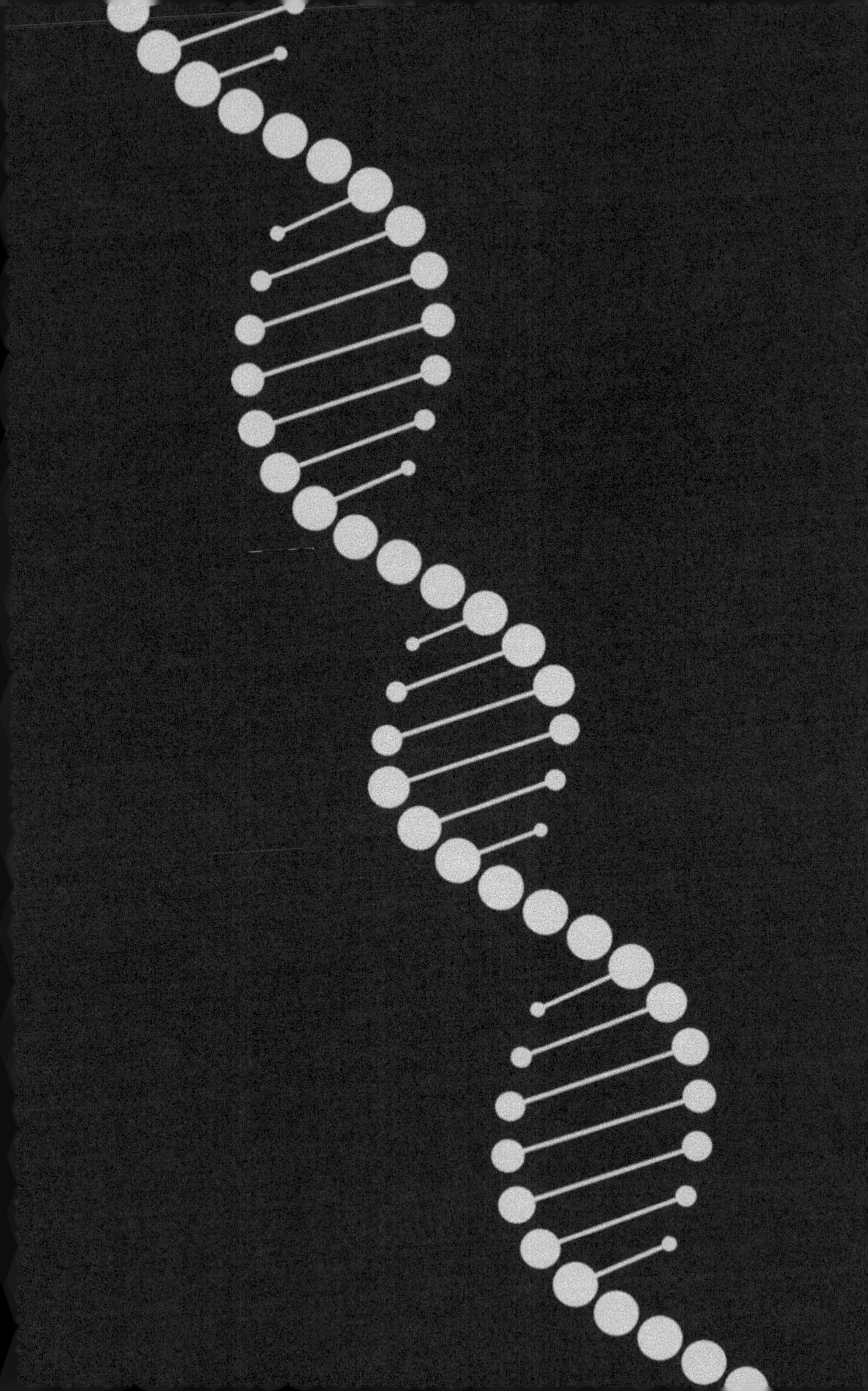

PART 3

Era of Tobacco Mosaic Virus

CHAPTER 14

Brilliance at Birkbeck

The intensity was what everyone who met her recognized.

—ANNE SAYRE

1953, Birkbeck at University of London

On March 18, 1953, Rosalind took her Turner and Newall fellowship grant and transferred to Birkbeck College, less than 2 miles (3.2 km) away in the Bloomsbury district of London. The atmosphere at the Birkbeck lab was upbeat. That was a credit to J. D. Bernal, who was "a big enough man to allow people [their] independence." Bernal, nineteen years Rosalind's senior, had pioneered X-ray diffraction and in the 1930s analyzed the first X-ray diffraction pictures of the protein, pepsin. He and Dorothy Hodgkin advanced many of the X-ray diffraction theories Rosalind had been introduced to in Paris. Rosalind was pleased to work with Bernal, and Birkbeck was also where Werner Ehrenberg and Walter Spear had produced an X-ray tube that rivaled no others. She'd used their

Franklin's lab at Birkbeck College (photographed shortly after her death) was on the fifth floor of a bomb-damaged eighteenth-century townhouse in Torrington Square, in the former maid's quarters. Her X-ray equipment was in the basement, in what had been the kitchen. The building has since been torn down.

high intensity X-ray tube to make her camera at King's and to photograph DNA.

From the outside, Rosalind's new workplace felt eerily reminiscent of the time she first approached King's College. Two years earlier, she had walked around the bombed-out crater in the middle of King's courtyard to get to her lab. Birkbeck College's Biomolecular Structure Laboratory numbers 21 and 22 were two redbrick converted houses on Torrington Square that had not yet been rebuilt after bombing from World War II. Almost a decade had passed since the end of the war, but reminders still touched everything and everyone in London.

Rosalind came to Torrington Square looking for peace. "I shall be moving from a palace to a slum, but I'm sure I shall find Birbeck pleasanter all the same," she said. Rosalind's lab was in the basement of 21 Torrington—a place that had been a kitchen—and her office was at the very top of 21—a place that had served as the maid's quarters for the house. Four flights of stairs separated her lab and office, and the last part of the stairs twisted in a tight circle. The office was an attic room with a leaky roof. Anne Sayre visited her at Birkbeck on a rainy day and was taken aback to see that "Rosalind had beakers and

The Lore of Torrington Square

People seemed to have been fighting or warring on Torrington Square forever. Legendary duels had taken place there in the late 1700s to early 1800s. Citizens christened it the Field of Forty, after two brothers died while fighting and left forty impressions of their feet on the field. The grass never regrew on those forty spots or on the places their bodies had fallen.

The 1800's lore was about two brothers that dueled for a "lady's" hand. Knowledge of the event has passed from generation to generation, and it is told like this . . . they met in the middle, paced away from each other, both brothers turned and fired immediately hitting each other. It has been said that the brother's footprints, forty in all, remained imprinted on the land keeping grass from growing in those spots as well as where the brothers fell to their death. The "lady" who lost two potential suiters is not discussed in this story. Some have counted more than forty footprints.

pots neatly arranged to catch the drips" to protect her desk and journals.

John Bernal

Despite the subpar accommodations, the personal working conditions were a huge, and happy, relief to Rosalind. Next door, at number 22 Torrington, was Bernal's office and residence. Bernal claimed the entire upper floor and entertained people from both outside and within the science community. Bernal's nickname was Sage because of his broad range of connections and his seniority as a scientist.

Something interesting was always bound to happen when Bernal was around. He attracted wild projects as well as fascinating people. Visiting her new boss, Rosalind eyed the mural of an angel and a devil drawn on his office wall. In 1950 Pablo Picasso had attended a party in Bernal's flat, and toward the end of the evening Bernal asked him for a drawing. He responded, "No, I'll do it on the wall." Using a multicolored grease crayon, he stood on a chair to reach above Bernal's books and drew the mural on the plaster.

While they were kindred spirits in science, Rosalind didn't mirror Bernal's personal beliefs. Bernal was no longer a handsome youth, but he still had a wicked smile and a wild head of hair. He and his wife, Eileen, had an open marriage, and it suited both for the entirety of their marriage—almost fifty years. He had another son with Margaret Gardiner and was renowned for his flirtatious behavior, having at least two mistresses including Dorothy Hodgkin. Rosalind never gave him any encouragement. In turn, he respected her genius and left her to her research.

Rosalind was to study tobacco mosaic virus at Birkbeck, with an eye to understanding the position of ribonucleic acid (RNA) in the virus. Because RNA acts like a catalyst, making things happen inside a molecule, she needed to understand the entire structure of the virus, including the position of RNA within the molecule.

Up until the 1890s, infected tobacco leaves were assumed to be dying from an unknown bacterium. Crops were curling and infected, their leaves discoloring in a mosaic pattern. In 1892 Dmitri Ivanovsky, a Russian botanist, discovered that it wasn't bacteria eating into growers' profits. Ivanovsky strained the harmful material through a Pasteur-Chamberland filter.

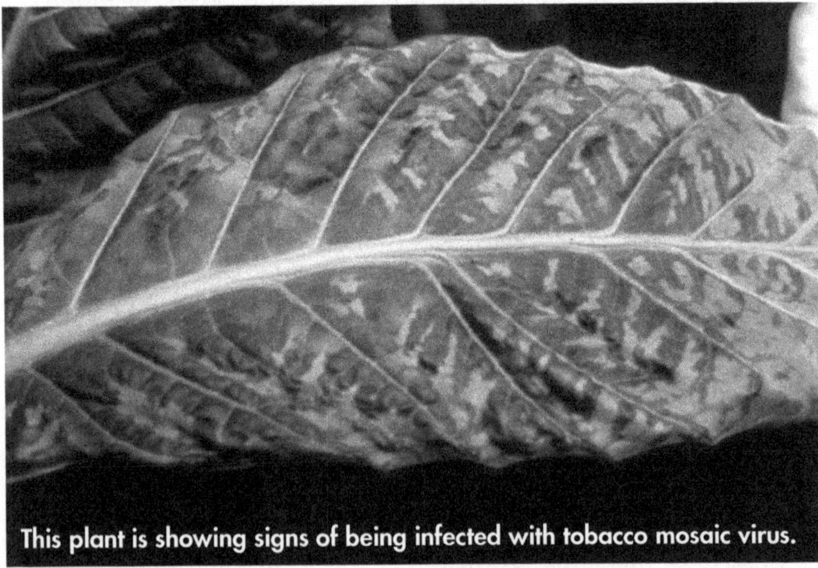

This plant is showing signs of being infected with tobacco mosaic virus.

If it were bacterial, it would have separated during filtering, but it did not. Something different was killing the plants. So, what was it?

Six years later, a microbiologist and botanist named Martinus Beijerinck realized that Ivanovsky's samples were highly infectious and could replicate among living plants. Beijerinck coined the term "contagium vivum fluidum," Latin for "contagious living fluid," which was shortened from "vivum" to "virus." TMV was therefore the first known virus.

Working with contagious plant viruses proved difficult over the next fifty years. Viruses could not be handled or treated the same as bacteria, and they were difficult to study because they were smaller than bacteria. Wendell Stanley, in 1935 and 1936, reported "needle-like crystals" in TMV that were extremely infectious and concluded they were protein. In 1937 Frederick Bawden and Norman Pirie, who both trained in virology, purified TMV by removing and separating the virus from the cells and calculated that the virus was comprised of 5 percent RNA molecules and 95 percent protein molecules. A year later, Bawden and Pirie experimented with the tomato bushy stunt virus and learned that it formed true crystals and contained closer to 15 to 20 percent RNA. They observed rod-like particles in the TMV molecule.

The two scientists observed the chains and individual protein molecules and labeled them subunits. Bawden and Pirie made another observation: Freezing the virus created a less potent sample. That year Bernal and Isidor Fankuchen took X-ray images and discovered that the virus particle was a highly ordered structure. But, having reached the limits of technology in the 1930s, they couldn't discern a repeating pattern.

During Cavendish's 1952 DNA moratorium, Watson worked on TMV and produced X-ray patterns much like those of Bernal and Fankuchen. Watson saw that TMV's diffraction pattern was helical and offered approximate measurements of the protein subunits. But Watson found the TMV diffraction research uninteresting, and his measurements were off because he based his calculations on the wrong reflection within the X-ray.

Now at Birkbeck and with a different scientific focus, Rosalind leaned into the past sixty years' worth of successes and struggles with TMV and plant virus studies. She set her research toward the shapes and angles of the subunits within the helix. Was RNA in the middle of the helical structure that Watson had observed, or was it found inside the proteins themselves? She'd need to understand whether the nucleic-acid-protein complexes were a double strand like DNA, whether RNA formed a single chain, or whether they were in different places inside the molecule.

DNA and TMV both replicate their structures, which allows viruses to spread easily, leading to contamination. But the biggest obstacle was that the structural unit of the TMV particle was too large to see the positions of all the atoms within one crystallographic X-ray image. Studying TMV required more work and care than studying DNA, and this difficulty kept many from studying TMV. Scientists in the early 1900s worked around the issue by grinding up the crystal and substituting the resulting powdery substance for the entire crystal. TMV was studied by examining a capillary tube filled with powder made of masses of tiny crystals with different orientations. X-rays of this type of material were known as powder photos.

Rosalind's love of the sciences was reinvigorated with this new project. She was confident she could tackle the issue without resorting to powder photos. Investigating viruses as a three-dimensional structure in its original form was paramount. To study diffraction of TMV, Rosalind first needed to assemble a microscope much the same as the one she had designed and assembled at King's.

She was still constructing her lab equipment when Bernal sent a letter to Randall inquiring about borrowing Rosalind's old setup. Bernal wrote, "Rosalind believes that the camera is not in use at the present and is stored in one of your cupboards." Bernal scribbled a sidenote, "borrow or buy," onto the typed correspondence referring to the microscope.

Randall did not reply. Rosalind had moved on from King's, but Randall could not let go of his territorial feelings about DNA and his irritation with her over the fraught relationship she had with Wilkins that led to King's losing the DNA race. He wrote to her on April 17, 1953, and asked her not only to cease any DNA work but also to stop thinking about DNA. And to top it off, he wanted her to stay away from Gosling.

Rosalind ignored Randall's letter, brushing it off as the typical way King's handled matters. She would not stop thinking about the subject, nor did she share Randall's belief that it was a problem to engage with Gosling. Gosling had been writing his PhD under her guidance, and she would not abandon him while he was mid-thesis, especially when Randall had not assigned Gosling another thesis adviser. Rosalind and Gosling met often on the sly at her new office during the first few months she was at Birkbeck. Gosling completed his thesis in 1954, and he included that he was "Deeply indebted to Dr. R.E. Franklin." He did not thank Wilkins.

In September 1953, Watson moved to Caltech to work with Max Delbrück and became a senior research fellow in biology to study X-ray diffraction of RNA. Rosalind and Watson exchanged considerable correspondence during this time. Perhaps Watson was appeasing her, needing her peer review of their DNA double helical structure, but Rosalind had already acknowledged the Watson and Crick solution in her April paper.

After her move to Birkbeck, Rosalind visited Crick often at Cambridge to talk about RNA and virus structure. Rosalind now could see in Crick the "gravitas, demeanor, and acute reasoning she expected of a great scientist." A friendship grew between her and the Cricks, particularly with Francis Crick's half-French wife, Odile. The two scientists developed respect for each other, and she'd jokingly scold Crick during their scientific debates, saying, "Facts are facts, Francis."

Was another race happening with TMV and RNA? Rosalind didn't think so. This time, information was flowing freely among the scientists.

As she began her TMV research, Rosalind encountered virus samples that were easily weakened by freezing just as Bawden and Pirie noted in 1939. She favored TMV that originated from Pirie at Cambridge, which Pirie gifted to Rosalind, assuming by doing so that she would never contradict his prior TMV findings. On November 23, a graduate student in Pirie's lab, Roy Markham, sent a package to Rosalind saying, "I'm sorry you are not having much luck finding TMV samples. I'm enclosing a specimen of TMV—which is very highly aggregated indeed. It is also as clean as or cleaner than the specimen which Watson used." Pirie's gift turned out to be both useful and troublesome.

Making these samples workable was tedious. Markham and Pirie had prepared them without a centrifuge, a process unimaginable in today's labs. Rosalind used dialysis bags to concentrate the specimens. She hung the bags on a string across the lab, like drying clothes on a line. She would squeeze

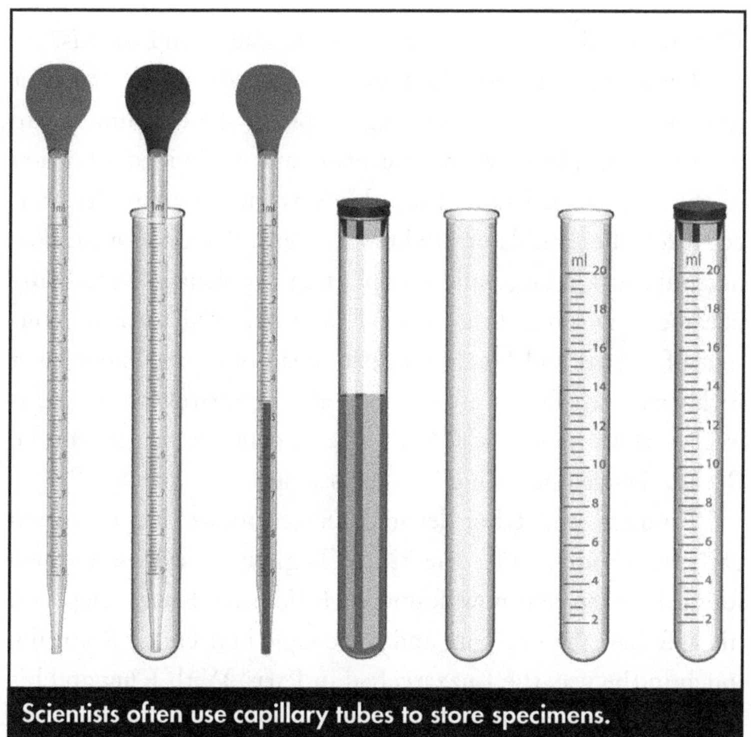
Scientists often use capillary tubes to store specimens.

the bags repeatedly to apply pressure until the sample material was thin enough to place into capillary tubes. Her goal was to study how water influenced the X-ray reflections on the TMV virus. Rosalind analyzed at least fifty specimens. She cultivated each of them and had to judge individually if they were usable.

Rosalind completed her first X-ray diffraction photographs of TMV by the end of the year. Rosalind indicated in her notebook, "RNA sensitive . . . easily damaged."

A new researcher joined Rosalind in the office next to hers on the top floor of 21 Torrington. Aaron Klug was twenty-six—six years younger than Rosalind—Jewish and a native of South Africa, and he arrived at Birkbeck in late 1953 with a Nuffield Fellowship grant to work on protein crystallography.

The two would prove to be great collaborators and friends.

Klug first ran into Rosalind on the attic stairs, and over time he watched the fascinating problems she encountered in her research. He noted her devotion and undivided attention to the science in front of her. He was more of a multi-project researcher and later credited her with demonstrating how he could tackle large and complicated problems. "I gradually became drawn into this work," Klug said, "and with the consent of Bernal and Harry Carlisle [head of crystallography at Birkbeck] transferred my interests almost entirely to the virus work." With plenty of TMV experimentation to go around, Rosalind enveloped Klug into her studies.

Rosalind and Klug debated science topics and perfected each other's ideas. The scientific collegiality that Rosalind had found in Paris she now found in Birkbeck's Klug. Klug and his wife had a young son, and the couple befriended Rosalind, much in the way the Luzzatis had in Paris. With Klug and his family, she returned to that Paris feeling: great science combined with friendship and a great mutual respect. "She *noticed*," Klug said. "She noticed everything." And, he added, "Her single-mindedness made her a first-class experimentalist."

CHAPTER 15

When You Disagree

Her choice was science. Her commitment to this choice was total; it was also joyful.

—ANNE SAYRE

1954, London and the United States

Rosalind was quite the sight when Bernal found her working under an umbrella in the basement lab, which was as damp as her leaky-roofed top floor office. Condensation from the ceiling pipes in the basement meant beads of water sporadically fell into her camera setup. While she wanted to add water to her TMV sample for X-ray diffraction, droplets from the ceiling weren't her idea of how to hydrate the specimen.

She'd finished building a special low-angle camera and was making progress varying the amounts of water in the specimens and recording the resulting differences in the diffraction patterns. Rosalind studied the interparticle distances and positions with different amounts of water to learn more about the center of the molecule—to understand if RNA was present in the structure's core.

Her initial studies and Fourier transform calculations did point to a heavy core, hinting at the presence of RNA. The diagrams she made from her efforts showed several hundred reflections suggestive of the helical symmetry in RNA viruses that other researchers had noted. Rosalind knew that the particles of the TMV molecule were structured in the shape of rods, as Bawden and Pirie had observed, and they'd also noted that in addition to proteins, the virus contained between 15 percent and 20 percent RNA. But exactly how much RNA was in the virus, where did it live inside the virus, and exactly how was the molecule structured? That was what Rosalind wanted to find out.

Money for research and salaries was a constant headache. Birkbeck, like many colleges and universities still do, relied heavily on grants for research. Rosalind's three-year fellowship grant from Turner and Newall was ending in March 1954. Rosalind applied to the Agricultural Research Council (ARC) for funding toward a "study of structures of plant viruses." Pirie assisted with her application. Rosalind asked for £1,100 a year from the ARC, and the grant was approved, although it was altered to £1,080—a difference of over $600 in today's currency. On principle, Rosalind found the modified salary upsetting.

By May, Rosalind needed extra computing assistance, to hand calculate several hundred reflections per image, and she couldn't do it alone. She was taking many images of TMV, each infused with different amounts of water to find the optimum preparation and orientation for the TMV specimens. So, Rosalind advertised

Shapes of RNA

A virus contains either DNA or RNA as genetic material. In most cases, DNA occurs in cells as a double-stranded helix, while RNA is single stranded. Double stranded means two complementary strands of nucleotides. Single stranded means one strand of nucleotides.

All RNA viruses have a capsid, a protein coat (shell) that protects its nucleic acid. RNA chains can fold up into a variety of shapes, either rodlike (helical) or spherical (icosahedral). Despite only one having the term *helical* as part of its description and name, all DNA and RNA are helical.

An additional difference can be if the virus is enveloped or not. Plant viruses are typically not enveloped, while animal viruses are enveloped.

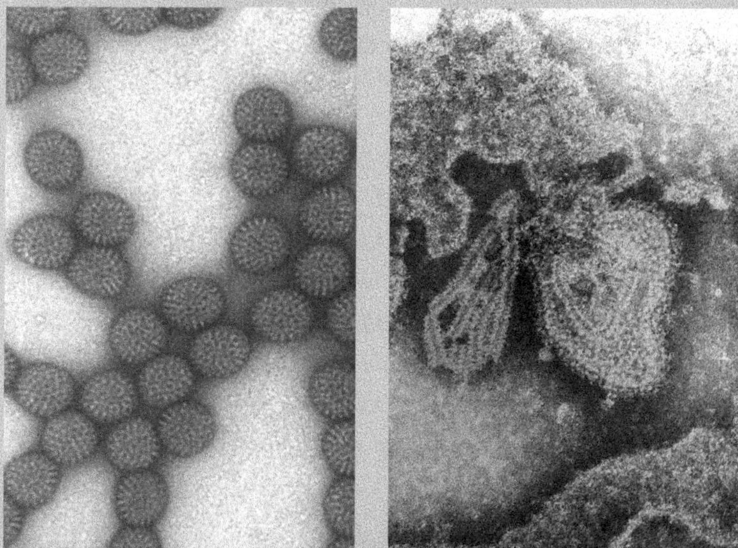

Left: Spherical particles of rotovirus. *Right:* Rodlike particles of mumps virus.

for a "computer"—a mathematically gifted person (usually a woman) who could perform a long string of calculations. She hired a Mrs. Piper, who could work at home for £25 a week, as well as Margaret Mitchell, who could work for £4,10.

Other financial considerations also pestered Rosalind. She was invited to speak on coal, on which she was still considered an expert, at the summer 1954 Gordon Research Conferences in New Hampshire. It would be her first trip to the United States. She also wanted to visit Berkeley in California to see Wendell Stanley, who ran a new Virus Laboratory, and meet with Pauling and Watson at Caltech. But first she had to find a sponsor to cover expenses for the trip. She obtained $700 from the conferences' organizers by bartering a visit to Penn State to give lectures at their labs in both Pittsburgh, Pennsylvania, and Cleveland, Ohio. The National Coal Board in Britain also threw in £250. Crick, still at Cavendish, reached out to Watson on her behalf, requesting funds. The correspondence from Crick to Rosalind was remarkably open:

> *Jim [Watson] and I talked to [Wendell] Stanley. He seemed interested (about TMV) and suggested he could pay part of your expenses.*
>
> *I was very pleased to hear about your TMV photos. Jim is certainly not doing any further work on TMV but is concentrating on RNA. His old idea for TMV was a helical arrangement of globular molecules (more or less) and as far as I know he has not developed this further.*
>
> *Yours ever, Francis [Crick]*

Stanley provided a fifty-dollar honorarium and boarding at the Athenaeum, a facility for faculty, in exchange for one lecture at Berkeley from Rosalind. Her trip was funded, but a hurdle remained.

Her initial visa application from the US embassy in London was questioned, whether she would be "gainfully employed in competition with American labor." Only after it was clear that her skill set was unique, and that she would be presenting papers on coal research as one of the world's leading experts, was her visa approved.

Rosalind's letters to her family during the entire trip are a travelogue of her impressions. Her transatlantic flight required four layovers. Reykjavik, Iceland, was dull, and she regretted falling asleep over Greenland and missed seeing the icebergs. Gander, Newfoundland, was nice and sunny, and she noted its flat landscape of scrubby grass, rock, and water.

Her first impression of the United States was not positive. "There is an overabundance of everything and the resulting complete self-confidence of individuals," she wrote. "Superficially they have everything and too much of it." And she added, "Meals are enormous, and consist mainly of protein and ice." And as to American accents, "I was puzzled by someone talking about the crocodiles she'd eaten, then discovered she'd said, 'hot dogs.'"

While the Gordon Research Conferences' focus was coal, she found the conferences more industrial than intellectual. From the conferences she traveled to MIT in Boston, Massachusetts, and met their specialist in nucleic acids, Alexander Rich, who had taken images of TMV. Rich then drove her to the Marine Biological Lab in Woods Hole, Massachusetts.

Watson visited Woods Hole while she was there. He was enjoying his first experience with celebrity after his DNA triumph, appearing in *Vogue* magazine and described there as "having the bemused look of an English poet." He was pleased to hear that Rosalind's X-ray diffraction of TMV confirmed his 1953 finding that subunits in the molecule were arranged helically. Rosalind was eager to share her TMV findings, and he was relieved (and perhaps surprised, again) when she didn't lash out at him. Watson even offered to drive Rosalind to California, but she had other plans—a cross-country tour by train.

She traveled to New York City, which she found uncivilized and rude. But while spending time with friends on a rooftop terrace with a view of Lower Manhattan, she admitted, "The sky-scraper group is surprisingly beautiful, and changes with changing light like mountain scenery." Then she was on to Philadelphia, where her opinions of the United States began to soften. In the field of fundamental biology, Rosalind said, "America is really leading and they have a remarkable number of first class people who form an elite group superior to any I have come across in England." Her excitement about the scientific advancements in TMV studies grew as she worked her way westward, giving lecture after lecture.

As she crossed the Plains and the Mountain West by train, she made stops including riding a mule to the bottom of the Grand Canyon. "I looked in vain for a hero to gallop in on a white horse," she said of a visit to an isolated ranch. Wherever she stopped, she expressed a fascination with the regional architecture. When in the Midwest, she wrote, "The front door opened into an enormous living room, as in medieval England." And finally in California, "The oldest influence in Southern California going back some 150 years is Spanish, and this has a pleasing effect on architecture, such as the stuccoed arches and red tile roofs." She continued to share her varied impressions of the United States with family, writing, "[Americans are] kind and well-meaning but incredibly ignorant and self-satisfied. On the other hand, the university scientists are as fine a crowd as I've met anywhere."

At Berkeley, Rosalind secured more samples of purified TMV and met with Wendell Stanley, Barry Commoner, and Heinz Fraenkel-Conrat, as well as geneticists and virus and botany researchers. At Caltech, she met again with Watson and realized that although he offered her a cross-country ride and helped find funds for her trip, he hadn't changed his misogynistic views. He and colleagues had formed the RNA Tie Club, described by Watson as having, "four honorary members and 20 regular members, one for each amino acid." The club was for men only.

But she did learn from Watson that a young crystallographer finishing his doctorate at Yale and about to move to Caltech, Donald Caspar, had found that TMV virus had a hollow core. That finding gave her pause. Where was the RNA? She didn't meet Caspar then, but the connection was made, and this connection would later prove significant both scientifically and personally.

All of these connections, scientific ideas, and questions would become the foundation for her next three years' work. In the short time that she was abroad, Rosalind's international scientific reputation had grown, starting with Crick's article on DNA in the October issue of *Scientific American*, in which he acknowledged her contribution. Crick wrote, "Watson and I were convinced that we could get somewhere near the DNA structure by building scale models based on the X-ray pattern obtained by Wilkins, Franklin, and their coworkers." Rosalind's Photo 51 was included, with credit to her.

Back in the United Kingdom that October, Rosalind received a three-page letter from Caspar, the young crystallographer now at Caltech, describing his TMV findings. Rosalind wrote back that she was preparing a paper on the topic and would have a draft to him shortly. By November she was working with Aaron Klug daily, as Bernal had given permission for their collaboration. Because the viruses among plants took physical form as either rods or spheres, it was decided that Rosalind would work on viruses that were rod-shaped and Klug on those that were spherical. Still, they needed additional help, so they advertised for assistants in the Appointments Vacant section of *Nature*.

Rosalind had not yet published anything on TMV. But she was able to make two observations about the virus's structure. First, the viral rods she saw in the photos were all equal in length. Second, the protein subunits that other scientists had observed inside the rods were identical. She wanted a colleague to review her findings before submitting them for publication in *Nature*, and the best person for this was Norman Pirie. He had supplied her with her first TMV specimens, and he had observed the rodlike shapes inside the molecule.

But Pirie was a difficult man, intemperate and proud, and Rosalind's findings contradicted some of his. He likely felt a false sense of ownership when it came to TMV. Between late October and November, Rosalind and Pirie exchanged several unpleasant letters. In a letter dated December 6, Pirie objected to many of her conclusions and itemized faults in her theories. Pirie's most biting words were, "Only those who did not realise that nature should not be assumed to be simple ever swallowed the hypothesis [that the protein subunits were all identical]. I suggest here that the idea of a single type of sub-unit is the least probable of all the possibilities—the runner up is that all are different."

Rosalind defended her position in a follow-up letter:

Dear Dr. Pirie,

Many thanks for your letter and criticisms, which were, as you suggest, not unexpected. In particular, I was afraid you would disapprove of the first sentence. . . . But the photographs . . . seem to show a convincing uniformity of length, indicate a fundamental unit of length 3,000 Angstroms. . . .

I hope that you do not disapprove so strongly of what I have written that you will never again be willing to provide me with material to work on. . . .

Yours sincerely,
Rosalind Franklin

The letter also contained her proofs and findings. Rosalind stuck to her observations and changed only the wording regarding the subunits by referring to them as "structurally equivalent." Perhaps she should not have mentioned the possibility of Pirie withholding future samples—because that's what he did.

Fortunately, Bernal, Rosalind's strongest advocate, allowed Rosalind and Klug to grow most of the samples they needed at Birkbeck. She had turnip yellow mosaic virus, tomato bushy stunt virus, and she later received additional tobacco mosaic

Sending Specimens Through the Mail

Rosalind swapped samples of viruses with scientists all over the world. Eventually, she received a form of purified potato virus, one virus that she had been desiring for some time now since it affected mainstream crops. The potato virus was known to be unstable, so she had to use it soon after receipt.

It was common among the scientists in the 1950s to send viral samples via postal mail, even across oceans. There seemed to be little consideration of safety protocols with these shipments. In one letter to Dr. Siegel, a California botanist, Rosalind wrote, "I regret to say that both tubes arrived broken, and there was no trace of any virus solution." She requested that he supply more, if he had any, presumably in the same manner.

That viruses of any kind would be shipped in such a casual manner would not only be intolerable today, but it would also be considered dangerous. Live viruses could easily spread if improperly handled. Today it would be considered as hazardous material and would be shipped as such.

viruses from Frederick Bawden, Pirie's colleague. Bawden also sent her purified potato virus, the cowpea strain of tobacco mosaic virus from infected tobacco plants and French beans, and specimens including the ribgrass strain of TMV.

A month later, Rosalind sent Bawden measurements showing "significant differences between the ribgrass and the common TMV strain." The result of her findings was that each virus had its own unique characteristics. Rosalind published these findings in *Nature* in 1955.

Her professional relationship with Crick had continued to bloom, and she ran a good deal of science past him. Rosalind often sent Bawden papers to review, and unlike Pirie, he returned helpful amendments. Watson approved of her *Nature* article and mentioned that Don Caspar also liked it. But Pirie, still a commanding force in the field, was bitter, and worked to have Rosalind's ARC fellowship grant recalled—the grant that he helped Rosalind obtain. It remained an open question whether he would be successful in any further vendetta against Rosalind.

CHAPTER 16

Defining Financial Moment

The position, there [at Birkbeck], is that I am paid and given facilities to work on my own ideas. . . . Its importance depends, of course, on what I make of it—what results I get, if any.

—ROSALIND FRANKLIN

1955, Birkbeck at University of London

Rosalind heard an enthusiastic "What's new?" coming from the stairs—Bernal's daily check-in. He was always interested to hear updates on the progress of Rosalind's TMV studies. Watson credited Bernal with the birth of molecular biology, and Rosalind recognized a small part of herself in Bernal. In the same way that Rosalind's mother had encouraged her, Bernal's mother, Bessie, enrolled him in science curricula rather than the traditional core courses. Bessie had only one rule: No experiments were to be performed in the house. Now Rosalind and Bernal were carrying out research trials on every floor of the 1800s era family home they used as a lab.

Rosalind's TMV research was progressing, but her relationship with Pirie was not. Her ARC grant—once championed by Pirie—was being squeezed. Pirie's bad temper amused Bernal, but he knew that Bawden and Pirie were very influential with the ARC. Bernal had to haggle over every item of new equipment and staff. Rosalind and Bernal were relying on the grant, but with Pirie's ire, their financial standing was rocky at best.

Rosalind documented what the Birkbeck department needed and why their requests were imperative to moving virus work forward. In a four-page proposal, she spelled out everything from the need for major diffraction equipment down to a single Hilger X-ray tube—the highest-quality X-ray tube on the market. The amount of work they could do would double if they could obtain a centrifuge. She also worried that funding for Klug's salary would expire.

Bernal sent her proposal to William Kershaw Slater, the secretary of the ARC, for approval. When Rosalind met with Slater, he did not appreciate the importance of Rosalind's work at Birkbeck. Worse, he quashed any possibility of using ARC funds for Klug's salary. Instead, Slater suggested that in two years' time, Rosalind should move to Cambridge to join Kenneth Smith's lab. He insisted it would be a simple move: one person and one X-ray tube. He didn't consider the value of teamwork nor the amount of time it would take to set up the needed equipment in a new location. When Rosalind pressed Slater on the move to Cambridge, he replied that her chances of staying at Birkbeck were slim to none.

Rosalind was angry. She said, "[Slater] appears to have

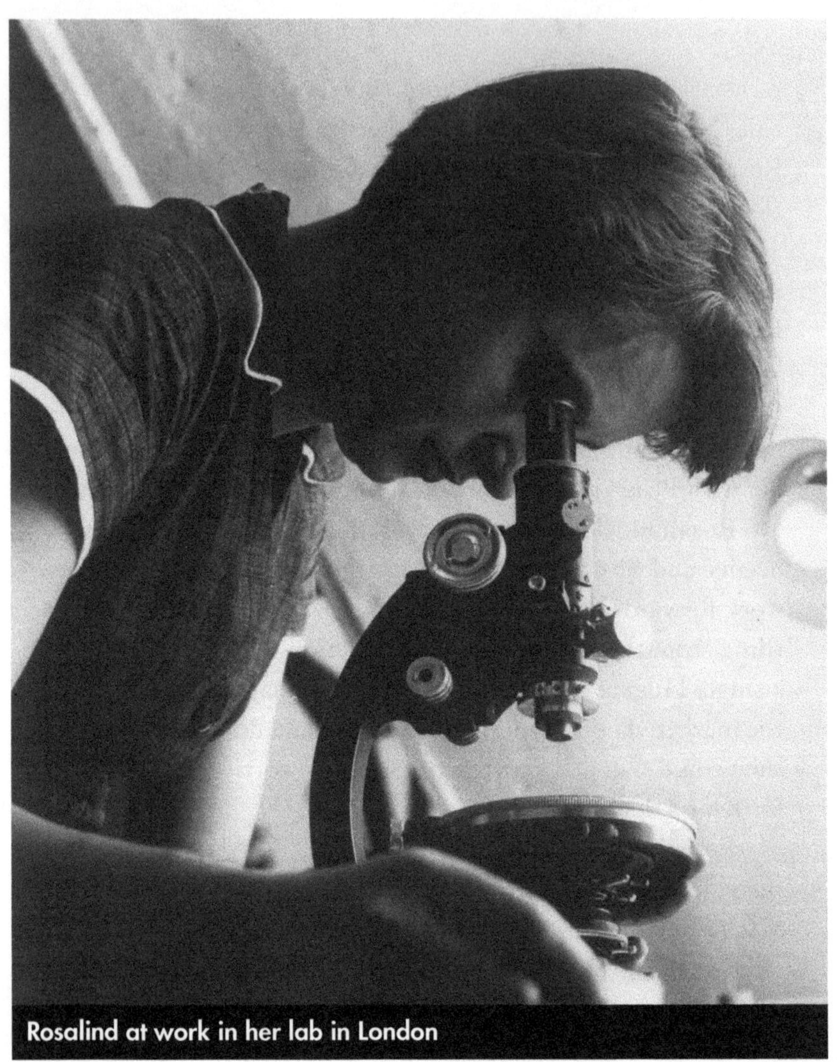
Rosalind at work in her lab in London

been badly upset by suggestion that ARC should provide lab space for work in a London university." He left Rosalind with the instruction to propose the need for a single X-ray tube. "The rest of my report," Rosalind said, "and request [were] ignored." Rosalind wrote a rebuttal letter. After explaining why moving to Cambridge was ridiculous, she requested that

Slater put her main points on the record.

Slater's stance seemed unfair even to Watson, who was watching from afar. He spoke up about the bias against Rosalind. Watson wrote a letter in Birkbeck's defense to Victor Rothschild, who was the chairman of ARC. Rothschild brought the matter back to Slater. But Slater again refused every one of Rosalind's requests. Klug said it was the only time he ever saw Rosalind in tears. Rosalind told him that she knew why they were denied funds: "It's because the ARC refuses to support any project that has a woman directing it."

Pirie's fury dealt Rosalind another blow. Over a year earlier Slater had talked to Rosalind of a promotion. "He told me," Rosalind reported, "that he would get something done about the question of transferring me from the grade of Senior Scientific Officer to that of Principal Scientific Officer." Now she wrote to Slater and reminded him that "similar assurance" had been given to Bernal. She said, "I should be most grateful if you would let me know what is the present position in this matter."

But Slater would not entertain this request either. He belittled Rosalind, calling her "my dear" and suggested that she ought to work under the constant guidance of a biochemist because otherwise she could not hope to understand the biological side of her work. "To reach that [Principal Scientific Officer title] at thirty-one," he told her, "would be only for the 'exceptionally distinguished.'" Slater's attitude was insulting, especially as she had garnered a high level of respect from other scientists for her work. Rosalind's 1955 and 1956 calendars were full of speaking engagements, at which she was often the only woman presenter.

Rosalind fought back. She sent a letter to Bernal: "The question of adjusting my salary to the new University scales has still not been settled. I have been doing full-time research continuously for the past 14 years and obtained my Ph.D. 10 years ago. I cannot believe that there is any rule which prevents the ARC from paying a salary greater than 1,080 pounds to a person of my age and experience." Her current salary was less than that of someone teaching or working in scientific civil service. The lack of employment security and her financial situation were unjust.

But some good news arrived in late spring. The advertisement Rosalind had placed in *Nature* for research assistants had paid off. Two young scientists came on board to write their PhD theses under Bernal, who set them to work with Rosalind. The first was John Finch, who had a physics degree from King's College. Finch began working with Klug on crystalline plant viruses. Rosalind had a good sense about collaborations and paired them well. Finch and Klug would continue to collaborate over the next forty years. The second, Kenneth Holmes, was a trained physicist at Cambridge. Rosalind worked with Holmes to identify what they referred to as "an equator of the pattern," the correct reflection point that had eluded Watson in 1952.

In the autumn of 1955 Don Caspar at Caltech also joined her at Birkbeck for a year as a postdoctoral fellow in molecular biology. He and Rosalind had not met except through correspondence. Caspar described seeing Rosalind for the first time and being taken aback. He had not expected her to be an attractive, vivacious young woman.

The two had a lot in common. Like Rosalind, Caspar was Jewish, intelligent, and focused on their research interests. Like the romantically naive Rosalind, Caspar admitted that he was inexperienced in matters of the heart. He later admitted he had "more rapport with Rosalind than with most of the men" he knew.

Caspar and Rosalind hit it off right away. "Hey, Ros!" he'd call out.

Although no one else could call her Ros, she did not mind Caspar's familiarity. "Somehow the young American got away with it," Ken Holmes said. "He was unmarried and had a disarming friendliness."

Rosalind was of course delighted that Caspar was also a first-rate scientist. He brought with him a Geiger counter unused since 1929 that he'd rescued from the Yale physics lab, something that had been on Rosalind's wish list. In early 1955 at Caltech, Caspar had used it to measure intensities of diffractions from TMV gels and had constructed the first radial density map of the virus.

Because of Caspar's earlier finding that TMV had a hole in the center of the structure where Rosalind assumed he should have found RNA, both were on the hunt to find the RNA. They began using a method of X-ray diffraction called heavy atom substitution, invented by Perutz and Kendrew. They added atoms of mercury to the protein in the virus at regular intervals to see more clearly the structure of the virus. The key was comparing X-ray diffractions produced by crystals of the molecules with and without the mercury. This led to Rosalind's next discovery: RNA winds around the inside of the protein units in a "helical groove," or indentation.

Rosalind's team demonstrated that the surface of a TMV particle was not smooth but had protrusions and bumps that corresponded to the individual protein subunits. They looked at many derivatives of the virus to arrive at this conclusion. The orientation of their particles was easier to see over time as they loosened up and "disaggregated." Rosalind nursed the samples to get them into their optimal viewing state. When she did, she could see that the proteins "stacked on top of each other in pairs to form a rod."

In addition to growing their own samples at Birkbeck, Rosalind and Caspar turned their expanding human resources toward the study of other viruses: the turnip yellow mosaic, the tomato bushy stunts virus, pea streak, and potato—all specimens that Rosalind had received from Bawden and others around the globe. In all, Rosalind and her team accomplished significant advancement in the X-ray diffraction studies of TMV, the location of RNA in a TMV molecule, and the structure of the turnip yellow mosaic virus. She determined that the RNA chains are embedded in the protein, a finding scientists had been seeking since the 1930s.

Rosalind used her 1955 annual ARC report to fight again for money to replace Klug's Nuffield grant that would soon end along with his salary. Despite Pirie's unhappiness that she was acquiring samples from other labs, Rosalind wrote about collaborating with other institutions on virus studies. She told the ARC committee, "We must remain dependent on the generosity of research workers overseas." She explained that if Klug wasn't placed on the ARC payroll, he would leave, and he was too integral to lose. And she leaned into the issue of the centrifuge in her report. The head of the ARC understood, yet the funding problems lingered.

Rosalind did end the year with some good financial news. On December 15, a letter from Birkbeck's clerk arrived. The salary adjustment that she'd requested back in July was approved and Rosalind's salary was raised from 1,080 to 1,200 pounds per year.

CHAPTER 17

Tough as Nails

She insisted on being daring.

—ANNE SAYRE

1956, London and the United States

Rosalind's coal and DNA research had inspired her to publish over sixteen papers in a span of less than eight years. She'd coauthored many with her research teams, and her virus studies were prompting a new spate of journal articles, this time with Klug, Holmes, Caspar, and Finch.

In March 1956, Rosalind presented at the Biophysics and Biochemistry of Viruses Conference in London. Rosalind knew all thirty-four male attendees, including Watson, Crick, Bawden, and Pirie. Rosalind presented a TMV paper she had coauthored with Klug and Holmes. In a post lecture roundtable, Pirie defended his theories. Pirie cited Bernal to give credibility to Pirie's premise that TMV particles had ridges and grooves. He asserted that more than one RNA strand could fit into the molecule. She defended her paper, saying, "It is not sure that there is more than one RNA strand [in TMV]." Watson and Crick weighed in on Rosalind's side. She won the debate, and Pirie would remain her enemy.

Robley Williams, a virologist from Berkeley, visited Rosalind's lab and was struck by their lack of basic equipment and offered a potential solution: Birkbeck's virus research might be aided by the US National Institutes of Health (NIH). Rosalind wondered why the United States would help fund a British research project, but she'd consider it. She also needed funds to attend the upcoming Gordon Conference in June. A Birkbeck administrator who supported Rosalind's position lamented how long it was taking for her to be promoted to reader and to be given a chair at the college.

The constant fight to fund her research, from equipment to positions to travel to salaries, was disheartening. But the number of scientists who spoke up in support of Rosalind attending the Gordon Conference was impressive. Wendell Stanley wrote to Bernal on February 7 to discuss the contribution that Rosalind would make. Bragg sent an application to the Rockefeller Foundation on her behalf on February 27, and on April 19, Rosalind received a grant from the Rockefeller Foundation for travel across the United States from mid-June to mid-August. She scheduled lab visits with scientists from the East Coast to the West Coast. She was determined to make the most of their generosity and belief in her.

Before leaving for the United States, Rosalind spoke at a symposium for the International Union of Crystallography concentrating on pure and applied methods in Madrid, Spain, a place she had not yet visited. She was excited. "I would be happy to go anywhere at all," she said to Adrienne Weill, "in the cities, to the seaside, to the caves at Altamira."

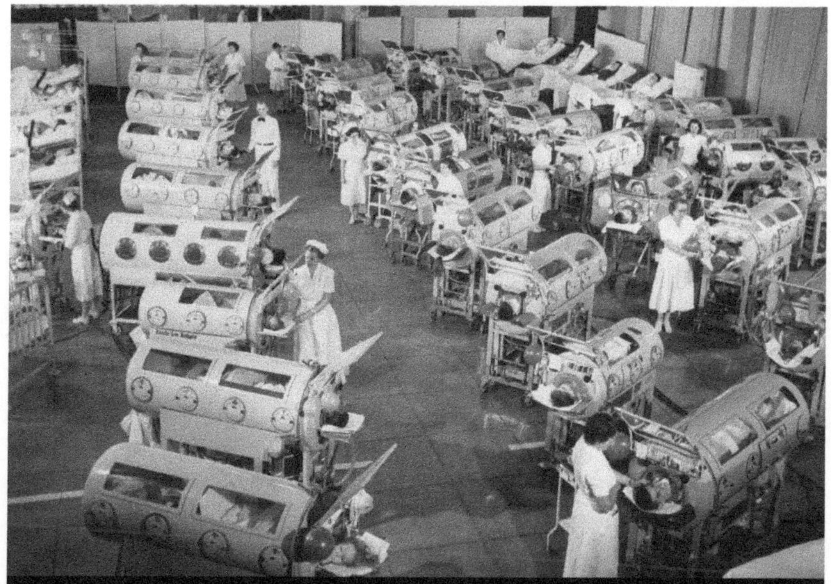

One of the symptoms of polio is muscle paralysis. Many people with the virus were placed in an "iron lung," which helped them breathe as they recovered.

When the symposium was over, Rosalind traveled with Francis Crick and his wife to the south of Spain. As one-third of the Crick traveling party, Rosalind got on with the couple well and especially with Odile. But Francis Crick later revealed that they learned almost nothing personal about her and did not know her intimately. "But," said Crick, "did anyone?"

Rosalind started her two-month US trip on June 16. Following the Gordon Conference in New Hampshire, Rosalind traveled to California and visited with Fraenkel-Conrat at Berkeley and Don Caspar, now back at Caltech. At Berkeley's Virus Lab, she met Fred Schaffer and along with scientist Carlton Schwerdt, they discussed using X-ray crystallography on poliovirus since polio was an RNA virus. This deadly virus was rampant in the 1900s, and survivors often were permanently paralyzed from the disease.

During her trip, Bragg asked Rosalind to participate in the Brussels World's Fair in 1958, a huge honor. Fair organizers wanted a model of TMV structure to be on exhibit in the International Science Hall, and Rosalind's model would represent Britain. This request kicked off a frenzy of work to build a 5-foot-tall (1.5 m) virus model to present to the world.

Before she returned to England, Don Caspar invited Rosalind to visit his family home in Colorado Springs, Colorado. Her hosts in Berkeley, Ethel and Irwin Tessman, who were phage scientists and old friends of Caspar's, sensed that Caspar and Rosalind were forming a serious attachment. Ethel Tessman said, "Rosalind used to glow when she spoke about Don." The Tessmans were hopeful that Rosalind and Caspar would become a pair. Although Rosalind never spoke openly about him, Ethel Tessman became convinced that the two were falling in love.

Irwin Tessman concurred. "Most telling for me," Irwin Tessman said, "was the enthusiastic way he talked about her."

The Tessmans also spoke warmly about Rosalind and "found her joyful, full of optimism, physically very beautiful, delightful and generous."

But while she was still in Berkeley, Rosalind experienced some severe pain in her abdomen. After a third painful attack, Rosalind visited a doctor, who gave her painkillers and advised her to see someone as soon as she was back in the United Kingdom. She was fine with waiting. She'd rarely been ill since childhood, and her stoicism kicked in. She'd just hiked Mount Whitney. As with her experiences in the Alps, she wrote about that hike with eloquence and emotion: "Perhaps the most memorable moment of the trip was opening my eyes at dawn to see the great rocky mountain straight in front of me, with its thin pink line of sunshine along its summit." She did not want her trip cut short by this unexplained pain nor spend time in an American hospital.

Shortly before she was set to leave the Tessmans, Caspar's father died unexpectedly, and Caspar went to Colorado Springs to mourn with his family. When Rosalind wrote a letter of condolence to him, she expressed her desire to see him again before leaving the States. She repeated this desire three times in the letter: "I hope I shall see you."

In late August, she did. Despite his family's loss, Caspar wanted her to come to his Colorado home, and she wrote Klug, "I'm going to see Don after all." She spent a few days with him, hiking, picnicking, and touring the Rocky Mountains, and formed a good relationship with Caspar's widowed mother.

Rosalind told Anne Sayre much later that she'd met a man, meaning Caspar, that "she might have loved, might have married." But the pain she had been feeling in her abdomen spoke of something that would change her future.

CHAPTER 18

I'm All Right

We never discussed her illness. It's not a confiding sort of family; we were very private and we would not share emotions or thoughts or anything with each other at all.

—ROLAND FRANKLIN

Fall 1956, London

Once home in London, Rosalind saw Mair Livingstone, a doctor friend in Hampstead. Rosalind's stomach was so distended that she couldn't easily zip her skirt. Livingstone asked if she might be pregnant. Rosalind said she was not but added, "I wish I were." She would've then had a reason for the pain. Livingstone sent Rosalind to University College Hospital, where her doctor there marked her case file, "URGENT." Rosalind saw a surgeon the next day, August 30.

Then she went back to work and cleared her desk, sending off several long letters including trip reports to colleagues at Berkeley. She detailed how she had prepared gel specimens of

TMV and how one experiment was not a success but that she was optimistic because she found out how to get a sample ready for X-ray analysis without distortion.

On September 4, surgeons removed two tumors from Rosalind's abdomen. In the patient notes, the doctor wrote that one was the size of a "tennis ball" and the other the "size of a croquet ball." Sayre visited in the Obstetrical Hospital where she was recovering from surgery. Rosalind insisted that she would be fine and didn't mention the tumors. When Rosalind was strong enough to leave the hospital, her brother David picked her up and took her to their parents' home. Rosalind carried on as if nothing was wrong and kept in touch with her lab.

But the surgeon was not so optimistic. "The findings are most unfortunate," he reported. He called Rosalind's parents himself, telling her mother, "Your daughter has cancer." Muriel Franklin's anxiety over Rosalind's health and her tendency to hover had always been a sore point between them. Rosalind hid the serious side effects of her illness from her parents, moving back to her own flat as soon as she was able.

Rosalind didn't want anyone telling her that she couldn't work, and she needed to construct her model of TMV for the Brussels World's Fair. The model required a rodlike object to depict the subunits of TMV. Byron Wilson, a colleague, imagined a handlebar grip from a bicycle would be the perfect shape and ran to a nearby general store to purchase almost three hundred. The salesclerk called the manager, because "It could only be a lunatic who would ask for the shop's entire stock." But Wilson came back to the lab with the handle grips.

Ken Holmes watched this model under construction with a sense of humor, saying, "The finished structure looked exactly like hundreds of handlebar grips stuck into a cylinder of cardboard."

Aaron Klug stands in front of his model of TMV.

Rosalind reimagined their materials and had new display forms made from expanded polystyrene. Klug turned to a friend, sculptor John Ernest, to produce the hundreds of polystyrene TMV subunits. They left gaps in the model to show that the RNA, represented by a red plastic tube, wound around and between the subunits.

In increasing pain, Rosalind went back to the hospital and wasn't released until late October after undergoing a hysterectomy. Sayre worried, but Rosalind assured her friend that everything was fine. When Jacques Mering heard Rosalind was ill, he phoned from Paris, but Rosalind didn't speak with him while she was still in the hospital. Sayre took the call and described him as distraught. It was around this time that Rosalind revealed her feelings for Mering from the years Rosalind worked in his lab: "[I had] been very much in love with Mering."

She did not share her cancer diagnosis, telling colleagues and most friends that she was being treated for an infection, saying, "Please stop worrying about me—everything is going very well, and I expect to be fully back to normal some time next month." Back in her parents' house after her operation, Rosalind said to Sayre, "My mother seems to have understood that I not only don't mind being left alone at times but positively like it, so things are a lot easier than last time." But two weeks after she was out of the hospital, to avoid her mother's hovering worry, Rosalind left home to stay with Odile and Francis Crick.

Francis didn't know her full diagnosis. After staying with the Cricks for a time, she bunked with her brother before going back to her flat at Donovan Court.

Rosalind used her recovery time to work on her notes and kept in contact with Birkbeck. Her mind turned again to Birkbeck's money troubles. She decided that she'd exhausted all potential sources for funds in the United Kingdom. Remembering the advice she'd received from Robley Williams, she said, "We are now reduced to applying for American funds to carry us on!" Rosalind and Klug drafted a letter to the NIH outlining what their lab had accomplished and requesting funds for three years starting in October 1957. Rosalind would be principal investigator and Klug the coprincipal, and they described the equipment they needed to advance their studies. Williams offered Birkbeck his full support.

Rosalind's health continued to decline. By the end of 1956, getting to her office on the fifth floor became increasingly difficult as her illness progressed. But she also had moments when she felt well enough to travel and sought the company of good friends. While recovering from another surgery, Rosalind convalesced with the Luzzati family in Strasbourg, France.

1957

On January 1, Rosalind received a letter from Birkbeck. At thirty-six years old, she would be granted the title of honorary assistant director. She was now in a respected position with three outstanding colleagues at Birkbeck: Klug, Finch, and Holmes. And by elevating her, Bernal proved that he thought her a first-rate leader.

But that spring, the ARC offered Rosalind and her cohort only 4,300 pounds for one year. Klug's grant would run out in six months, and that amount didn't buy him a whole year of a low salary. Rosalind particularly wanted to secure support for him. Birkbeck also needed equipment. They were down to the wire.

On July 9, three months before Klug's grant ran out, the NIH awarded Rosalind and her team the largest grant that Birkbeck had ever received: 10,000 pounds per year. The grant ran for three years starting in October. She wrote to Sayre, "We are fixed up for the next 3 years and are extremely grateful to all you kind American tax-payers."

Don Caspar reappeared in Rosalind's life during summer 1957, traveling with his mother. The two stayed in Rosalind's flat. Rosalind didn't tell anyone that the cancer had returned and spread. She was positive that science would find a cure. Instead of wallowing in her condition, she took a summer holiday trip to Switzerland with the Caspars. The highlight of the trip, she told Sayre, was "a glorious weekend in Zermatt." She traveled back to Paris and Strasbourg, not to be hindered by her illness.

Francis Crick came to Birkbeck with a proposition. The MRC was constructing a new building at Cambridge. It would include a state-of-the-art Laboratory of Molecular Biology. Crick invited Rosalind's team to join this new lab. The team would no longer have to worry about renewing grants, borrowing equipment, and finding funds. This was all she had hoped for, and a testament to the value of her work and her legacy.

In May 1957 Rosalind attended an exhibition at the Royal Institution in London, to view the TMV model she and Klug had built. A gala was held on the evening of the last day of Rosalind's cobalt therapy cancer treatment. At the grand black-tie affair, she wore a red silk Chinese blouse. According to

Brenda Maddox, "No one who saw Rosalind in public would have guessed she was living under threat." Robley Williams gave a lecture, "Observations on the Architecture of Viruses." Then the audience wandered through the library to see four exhibits, including Rosalind's and Klug's model.

Rosalind's parents were invited to the gala. They came and found her "looking lovely, gay and happy." Rosalind did not complain or tell colleagues of her illness. She never uttered the word *cancer*. She remained committed to life and hopeful that a cure for her illness would allow her to finish her work on viruses and RNA.

CHAPTER 19

She Fought

She felt her mental power, and bitterly grudged its achievement being curtailed.

—ANNE SAYRE

1958, London

Between January and March 1958, despite her illness and treatments, Rosalind began to study poliovirus. Many researchers did not believe it was safe to have poliovirus in the lab. Werner Ehrenberg, the maker of the fine-focus cameras that Rosalind used for crystallography work, had been crippled by it. Others argued that the aging 150-year-old lab at Birkbeck wasn't the most sterile of facilities. According to Maddox, "Rosalind stored the [poliovirus] crystals in her parents' refrigerator" in a thermos, not a safe procedure.

The Salk polio vaccine developed in 1953 was newly available, and most of the members of her team were inoculated. Rosalind decided against getting vaccinated. Brenda Maddox did not believe Rosalind's vaccine stance came from the fact that she knew she was already quite ill, but more likely "that Rosalind, rather than manifesting an indifference to survival, was . . . conscious . . . of the low probably of an accident. She knew she wasn't going to drop or break the test tubes."

Rosalind and Klug later moved the virus crystals to the London School of Hygiene and Tropical Medicine and only brought polio crystals that were in capillary tubes to Birkbeck. Rosalind and Klug found that to study polio, they needed to use a different type of capillary tube than the standard ones they used for TMV. Poliovirus caused the original glass tubes to leak. Standard glass tubes are prone to corrosion. Klug and Finch switched to quartz capillary tubes, which are neutral and have an unreactive nature. This kept the leaching at bay and provided the best X-ray diffraction images of poliovirus to date. When Bernal saw the images, he said, "That photo's worth 10,000 pounds!"

Utilizing the NIH funds, the team hired a biochemist to help with the crystallization of poliovirus. The surprise, for the researchers, was seeing how similar the structure of poliovirus was to the plant viruses. Finch and Klug published this finding in *Nature* on June 20, 1959. Bragg requested that models of both TMV and polio be included in the Brussels World's Fair. Using the same model-building techniques on their poliovirus model as they had on their TMV model gave them a cohesive look.

For the next few months, Rosalind continued normal life as much as possible. She went to plays and exhibitions and dined out when she could. She arranged a celebration for her parents' forty-year anniversary and attended her father's birthday celebration.

The Royal Marsden Hospital specialized in treating cancer,

Rosalind Franklin in 1955

and when she was transferred there for treatment, it was the first time the other scientists on her team knew the extent of her illness. She was one of the first patients to receive chemotherapy at Marsden. This cancer treatment was fairly new, first used in 1951 at other London hospitals. Visitors "found her in a wine-coloured dressing gown, taking radioactive liquid gold in a tilting bed . . . with her sister Jenifer or one of her brothers by her side." Rosalind was convinced that the treatments she was receiving would keep her well until a cure for her cancer could be found. In January she signed another three-year lease on her flat and re-covered her couch cushions in bright colors.

In March she was working all day, albeit with less-than-optimal energy. Maddox said, "She would crawl up the narrow stairs from where the X-ray apparatus was, to her office on the top floor, refusing all offers to be carried as her devoted young associates longed to do. Her courage drove Ken Holmes almost to tears."

And perhaps it was more than courage. Was she in denial? Rosalind expected to recover, putting her faith in science. Vittorio Luzzati, visiting her in London, said, "She had a very strong will."

Anne Sayre added, "It was heartbreakingly plain that she was dying, but she seemed to [Luzzati] to fight this possibility every inch of the way. She never told him—or anyone, as far as he knows—what she was suffering from and made every effort to ignore even the obvious symptoms of illness." Sayre said, "I've known people in greater physical distress, but never in greater anger about the unwanted, inconvenient, unjust and cruel sentence of dying young. . . . She remained combative to the end."

In between her hospital stays, Rosalind chose to stay with her brother Roland and his wife, Nina, rather than with her parents. Rosalind wrote again to Don Caspar. She talked about the work with polio and mentioned her illness, but she said, "I still hope to come over this summer. If you felt like a trip West during August, it would be very nice if we could go over together."

An invitation to a six-month fellowship in Caracas, Venezuela, sat on the table next to her hospital bed, and she clearly had every intention of going. It was just the type of engagement she had been waiting for. All expenses—both living and travel—would be paid.

Jacques Mering visited Rosalind in the hospital shortly before her death. Anne Sayre said of his visit, "Her hair had gone white, and she had wasted away to a skeleton, but was insistently cheerful, and kept telling him . . . that she would get well."

Mering told Sayre, "She [Rosalind] was defying death itself." When Mering left Rosalind, he stood on a street corner in London and wept.

In her last letter to Don Caspar in mid-March, she wrote, "Although I am fairly well at the moment I have, in fact, been in hospital and out again since I got your letter. So it all depends how things go in the next few months."

On March 28, Rosalind produced five pages of calculations and completed the research for three papers that Klug later submitted for publication. Not including those papers, she'd authored thirty-nine publications on the microstructures of coal, DNA, and viruses. The TMV and polio models that Rosalind and colleagues built were erected at the World's Fair in Brussels, which opened on April 17. Rosalind missed the opening by one day.

Sayre wrote later, "She fought death with stubborn courage, made plans for living when the plans were a mockery. She died as she had lived, with a passion for life that she never relinquished. To this day, I miss her."

Rosalind passed away in Royal Marsden Hospital on April 16, 1958. She was thirty-seven years old.

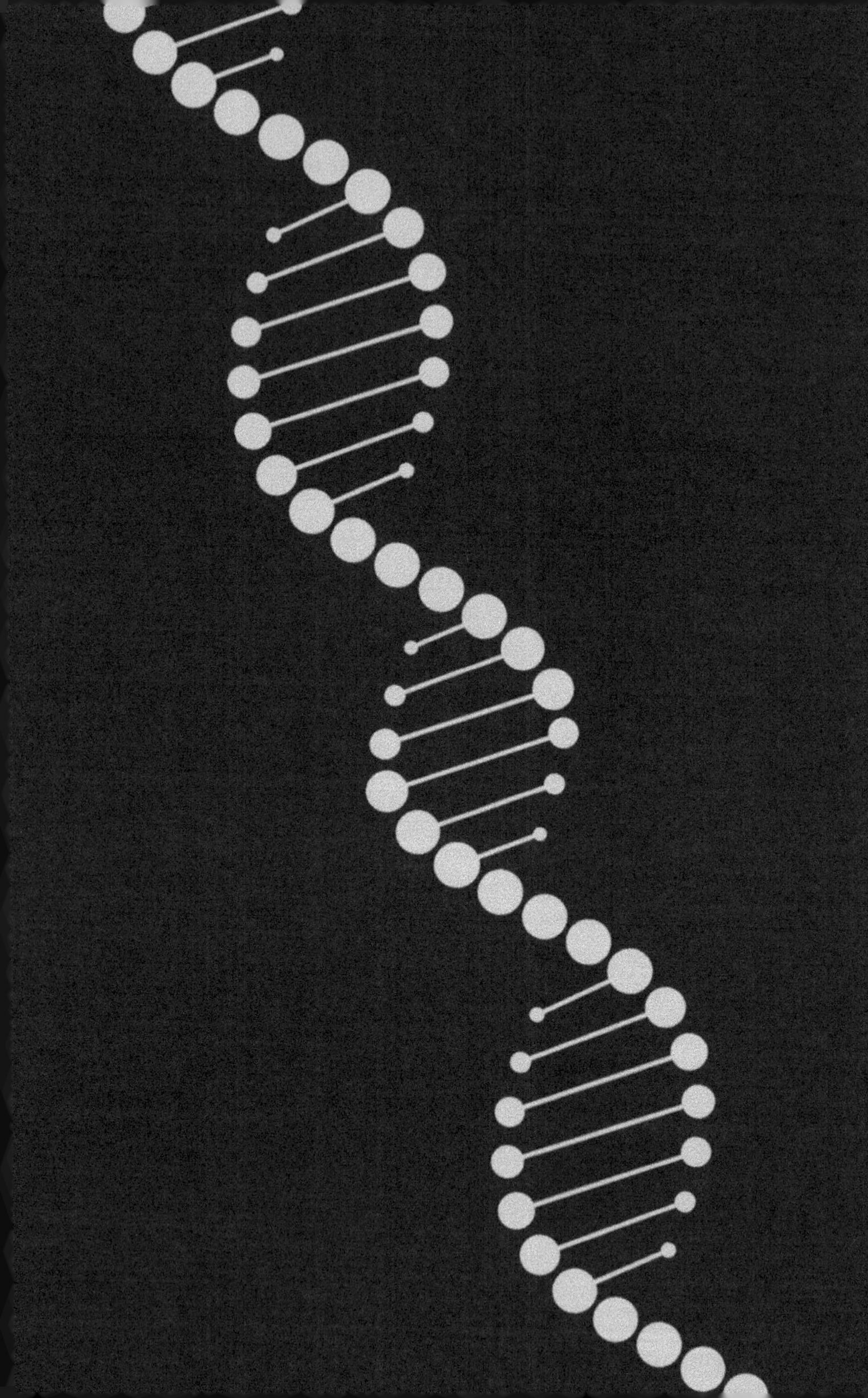

PART 4

The Story Doesn't End Here

CHAPTER 20

Rosalind's Goodwill and Contributions

Her work on viruses was of lasting benefit to mankind.

—ROSALIND FRANKLIN'S TOMBSTONE INSCRIPTION

1958, London

Despite her enduring belief in survival, Rosalind had made her will in December 1957. She named her three brothers as executors. None of her family members were beneficiaries. She knew it was not necessary to leave anything to them as they were all wealthy. Rosalind had always been embarrassed when the subject or implication of family wealth was mentioned.

She left Aaron Klug's family enough money to make a deposit on a new house, her Austin car, and 3,000 pounds. Brenda Maddox said of her generosity: "Next on her list were two close women friends who had children to support: for Mair

Livingstone, 2,000 pounds, for Anne Piper, 1,000 pounds. Last, 'my old Nurse Miss Griffiths' was to have 250 pounds." Any remaining funds were to be "distributed by the executors to charities of which they think I would have approved."

On learning of Rosalind's death, her research associates Ken Holmes and James Watt broke down in tears, and John Finch, unable to believe the news, crept into a nearby church. Her stubbornness and stoicism had fooled them all into thinking she might survive. Vittorio Luzzati, already in London, attended her funeral. She was buried in the Franklin family tomb in Willesden Jewish Cemetery, London. The colossal number of exposed lab X-rays Rosalind had performed were never named as the culprit for her illness.

Rosalind never made much fuss about her career to her family, who were stunned to learn after her death of the details of her contributions. Her aunt Alice wrote to Sayre a week after

X-ray Exposure and Cancer

Not long after the discovery of X-rays and their initial use in medical applications, adverse effects such as cancer, were noted in higher incidence among those using this new technology. Due to increasing recognition of these serious consequences, the scientific community has led many protectionary efforts to limit unnecessary exposure of X-rays to those who work with them. Protections such as lead shielding, improvements in dosimetry—the measure of radiation an individual or tissue encounters—and increased knowledge have all made the use of X-rays safer in the modern era.

Rosalind died, saying, "She was very modest and also knowing it was Greek to us—she did not waste time talking about her work with those who would irritate her by silly questions."

Her sister, Jenifer, wrote, "Aware of our scientific ignorance, Rosalind did not communicate much about her work. It was perhaps not until she wrote home from America, from a Gordon Conference in 1954, that the family realized the importance of what she had been doing."

Bernal wrote her obituary, published in *The London Times* on April 19, 1958. He opened with this: "Rosalind Franklin's early and tragic death is a great loss to science."

July 25, 1930–April 16, 1958

Rosalind's contributions to humanity and science remain inspirational. Between Rosalind's research at BCURA and at the Paris lab, Bernal wrote in her obituary, she "discovered the fundamental distinction between carbons that turned on heating into graphite and those that did not. Further she related this difference to the chemical constitution of the molecules from which the carbon was made."

In two years and two months at King's, she assembled an Ehrenberg fine-focus X-ray tube with a Philips micro camera for taking high-resolution photographs of single fibers of DNA. Springboarding from the single fiber camera, she later assembled a second micro camera, and called it a tilting camera, to photograph specimens inclined to the X-ray beam at a series of angles. This was paramount to applying the Fourier and Patterson mathematical formulas to Rosalind's and Gosling's images.

Her research unveiled the existence of two structural phases of DNA using imaging. Both the A-DNA and the B-DNA structural forms originated from the same sample, a crystalline form obtained at 75 percent relative humidity and

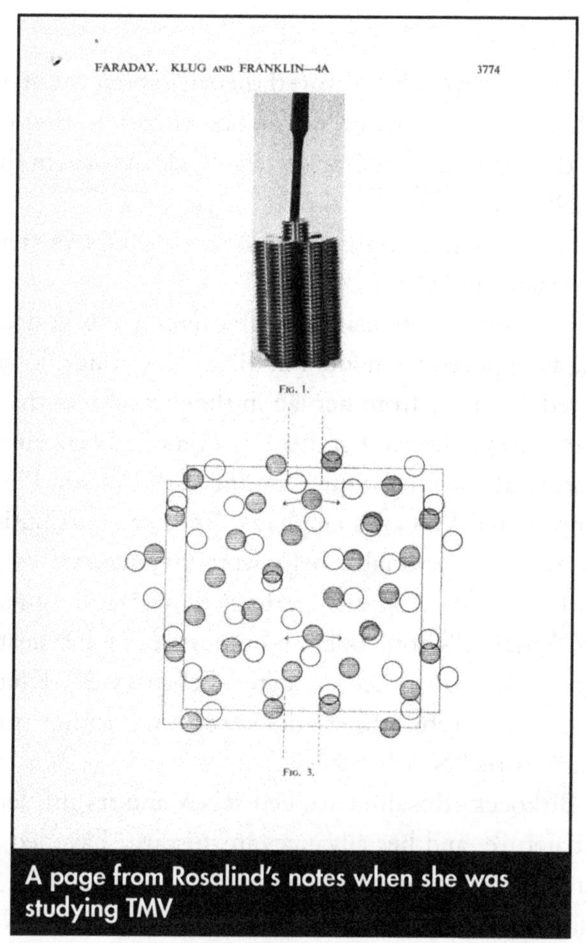

A page from Rosalind's notes when she was studying TMV

a new structure showing a lower degree of crystalline order—a paracrystalline structure that persisted for a wide range of humidity. She also demonstrated that the transition of A-DNA to B-DNA form was reversible. Klug stated that her "careful, systematic experimental work . . . made possible the characterization of the two states of DNA."

She realized that any correct model of DNA must have the phosphate groups on the outside of the molecule. Her analysis of diffraction patterns of the two forms of DNA was the evidence that proved or disproved theories about the structure of DNA. She applied helical diffraction theory to the A-DNA form in the last half of 1952 and to the B-DNA form in the first part of 1953.

She came tantalizingly close to solving DNA's structure before Watson and Crick.

Her insistence on using the Patterson method on the A form, as opposed to model building, slowed her down. She contracted flu, away from her lab in the pivotal months of scientific discovery, December 1952 to January 1953. Her stubborn nature alienated Wilkins, and he gave Watson Photo 51, which prompted Watson's epiphany. But her contributions to the discovery of the double helix were documented by Aaron Klug, who was her last and perhaps closest colleague. Klug received Rosalind's notebooks and reports upon her death. On the page in her lab notebook dated February 23, Klug later annotated her careful observations, referring to her notes on DNA structure: "Nearly home."

At Birkbeck, Rosalind studied RNA and its influence on virus structure, and her advances in this area have led to our current understanding of virology. Had she lived, she would have made further strides in research on poliovirus, RNA, and likely much more.

Long after the struggles Rosalind suffered at King's and well after her death, her ability to collaborate bore fruit. In 1960, Klug, Holmes, and Finch moved Rosalind's lab to Cambridge to join Crick's new Laboratory of Molecular Biology. Bernal recognized her spirit of collaboration and ability to bring skilled researchers into her orbit in his obituary, "as the small and devoted team she gathered round her bears witness."

Rosalind's remarkable contribution to science should not be forgotten.

CHAPTER 21

A Noble Nobel?

Of all crimes the worst
Is to steal the glory . . .
Even more accursed
Than to rob the grave.

—ROBERT FROST POEM THAT ANNE SAYRE ASCRIBED TO ROSALIND

December 1962, Stockholm Concert Hall, Sweden

During the race to discover the structure of DNA, the prospect of winning the Nobel Prize in Physiology or Medicine, the world's top scientific award, had been all consuming. The rival scientists in the United Kingdom and the United States had thrown ethical considerations and past agreements out the window. These scientists were willing to do anything to seize this career-changing opportunity.

On December 10, 1962, four years after Rosalind's death, James Watson, Francis Crick, and Maurice Wilkins were awarded the prize for the discovery of the three-dimensional structure of DNA. The ceremony was a staid and formal affair in the Stockholm Concert Hall in Sweden. Following a musical interlude, Arne Engstrom, a professor of physics in Sweden, introduced the three recipients. Swedish King Gustaf VI Adolf presented the medals to each of the three men.

Observing the ceremony in photos and videos is telling, particularly with respect to Wilkins. Once he was seated with his medal, Wilkins's shoulders rounded, and he turned away from his fellow recipients. It's easy to assume that his emotions swirled between pride and guilt. Rosalind Franklin was likely much on his mind. She should have been on the stage receiving the highest honor science can bestow. James Watson was candid on this point in his 1968 book, *The Double Helix*: "The long-standing rule that a Nobel Prize can be shared by at most three individuals would have created an awkward if not insolvable dilemma had Rosalind Franklin still been alive."

Years later, Wilkins concluded, "The DNA story was driven by strong emotion, and all the main characters did things which, from the outside, might appear discreditable, even despicable." He said, "[It was] such a very great scientific advance and what a pity that tempers frayed, and jealousies arose. . . . How can humans escape such feelings?"

James Watson's book *The Double Helix* was published ten years after Rosalind passed. While it was a best-selling book, it met with harsh reviews from colleagues, friends, and family because of the unprofessional and dismissive way Watson talked about Rosalind and the lack of credit he gave to her work. The book made those who knew her and knew of her reputation uncomfortable.

In his interview with Sayre, Jacques Mering said, "This version of history [in *The Double Helix*] is a little too personal to be history. Besides, Rosalind Franklin—whom I knew well—bore no resemblance whatever to Watson's grotesque."

And Sayre believed that "the Cambridge people were less than ethical (shall we say?)."

Maurice Wilkins was also upset by the details revealed in *The Double Helix.* Watson said, "As soon as Max [Perutz] saw the sections by Rosy and Maurice, he brought the [MRC] report into Francis and me."

As for sharing the photograph with Watson, Wilkins said, "I had been rather foolish to show it to Jim during our hurried conversation in the corridor." Had Wilkins been more of a colleague to Rosalind, the Nobel Prize for the discovery of the three-dimensional structure of DNA might have been awarded to a different trio.

Wilkins's final years were spent in his small office. Above his desk he'd hung a print of a ballerina who reminded him of Rosalind. Wilkins said in an interview, "[Rosalind] gave me the impression of being nimble—moving lightly like a dance. I had on my lab wall an old print of [ballerina] Carlotta Grisi in a graceful stance; years later I sometimes ironically and sadly referred to it as a picture of Rosalind. In dark times, in 1952, I sometimes felt Rosalind was lighthearted, contemptuous and amused by outwitting me."

Ballerina Carlotta Grisi dances *La Péri* in this painting. Wilkins had a copy of it in his office.

These men's complicated feelings about their choices came too late to have any impact on Rosalind. But the discovery that outlived her had become part of her legacy, whether her role was fully acknowledged or not.

What kind of legacy would Rosalind have chosen for herself? A letter to her father written in 1942 may provide a clue: "My method of thought and reasoning is influenced by scientific training . . . [science] is based on fact, experience and experiment. . . . By doing our best we shall come nearer to success and that success in our aim (the improvement of the lot of mankind, present and future) is worth attaining."

Rosalind's Colleagues

King's College Biophysics Lab

Raymond Gosling (1926–2015)

Gosling was a crystallographer who joined King's College in 1951 and was working with Maurice Wilkins on imaging DNA when Rosalind joined the lab in 1952. Randall assigned Gosling to work closely under Rosalind on X-ray diffraction. Rosalind was also assigned as Gosling's thesis adviser as he worked toward a physics PhD.

Notable work: Gosling took an important X-ray diffraction image right before Rosalind joined King's lab. It proved that DNA could be crystallized. Many consider Gosling to be the first to crystallize genes, but, in 1938, Florence Bell had also taken such an image. Her image couldn't show the clarity of Gosling's, and his crystallization photograph of DNA led to further groundbreaking discoveries. Furthermore, Gosling was by Rosalind's side when the famous "B-DNA" photograph was taken.

Connection to Rosalind: Gosling met Rosalind when she started working at King's in 1951. Gosling described Rosalind as having a positive personality, and he was excited to work with her and felt she was a great experimentalist. Gosling appreciated that Rosalind continued to help him finish his thesis on the sly after she left King's for Birkbeck College.

Other work: Gosling lectured at Queen's College in Scotland, then at the University of West Indies. Eventually, he moved toward developing equipment to diagnose atherosclerosis. In 1967 he became a lecturer and reader at Guy's Hospital Medical School, and then professor and professor emeritus in physics as applied to medicine. Later, he was involved in developing doppler ultrasound.

John T. Randall (1905–1984)

Randall was a physicist and was at the forefront of change as he turned his efforts toward biological questions. He established the Medical Research Center Biophysics Unit at King's College and hired Wilkins, Gosling, and Rosalind. Some described Randall as authoritarian and having a Napoleon complex. Gosling referred to Randall's unit as a "circus." But Gosling admired Randall and believed that his drive and vision were the qualities that led to the discovery of the double helix.

Notable work: Randall's early career involved the advancement of microwave radio energy, and he worked on a device that converted magnetic currents into heat; this magnetron changed the course of the war via enabling airborne radar systems.

Connection to Rosalind: Randall hired Rosalind to research proteins and then changed her assignment to study the structure of biological fibers [DNA] using X-ray crystallography with Gosling. Randall did not share this assignment change with Wilkins, who previously worked alone with Gosling. Many, including Wilkins and Gosling, believe that Randall's lack of communication with his team caused great animosity in Wilkins (toward Rosalind).

Other work: Randall moved to the University of Edinburgh and led a group on new biophysical methods. He was knighted in 1962 and elected a Fellow of the Royal Society of Edinburgh in 1972.

Maurice Wilkins (1916–2004)

Wilkins, a New Zealand born–English biophysicist, joined King's College in 1946 under the direction of Randall. Wilkins worked with Gosling on microscopes and imaging until Gosling was assigned to continue work with Rosalind. At this time, Wilkins started visiting another lab, Cavendish at Cambridge University, and shared King's information with James Watson and Francis Crick.

Notable work: During World War II, Wilkins worked on radar and isotope separation at the Manhattan Project at Berkeley. Then, at the University of St Andrews, he was the chair of the Physics Department. He then landed at King's College to work in their Physics and Engineering Departments. He won a 1962 Nobel Prize in Physiology or Medicine.

Connection to Rosalind: Wilkins and Rosalind met at King's. Despite the friendly first impression, things soured when he saw Rosalind as a threat when she took over his work on DNA. Their relationship became even worse as time went by, although after her death he expressed some remorse.

Other work: After receiving the Nobel Prize, Wilkins remained at King's College, directing its MRC.

Cavendish College Lab

Francis Crick (1916–2004)

Crick was a British molecular biologist who worked with Watson at Cavendish lab at Cambridge, which was competing against King's College. Both Cavendish and King's labs were funded by the MRC.

Notable work: Crick studied the art of x-raying polypeptides and proteins for his thesis where he received his PhD under Max Perutz. He won a 1962 Nobel Prize in Physiology or Medicine.

Connection to Rosalind: Crick often went to King's lab, and Rosalind knew Crick from many conferences. Crick never did any experimental [X-ray crystallography] work on DNA. He believed the way to solve DNA's structure was to build models. Crick used Rosalind's data, given to him by Wilkins, to build a model of DNA, which led to a Nobel Prize. Crick and his wife Odile became close to Rosalind and spent time with her in the months before her death.

Other work: Crick stayed at the University of Cambridge. Later in life, Crick researched theoretical neurobiology in his attempt to advance the scientific study of human consciousness.

James Watson (1928–)

Watson, an American molecular biologist, geneticist, and zoologist, worked with Crick at Cavendish lab at Cambridge, which was competing against King's College. Both Cavendish and King's labs were funded by the MRC.

Notable work: Before Cambridge, Watson did his postdoctoral research at Copenhagen University in Copenhagen, Denmark, where he was interested in nucleic acids and phages. At Cambridge, Watson's work concentrated on DNA. He approached uncovering the structure of DNA by building models. After receiving the Nobel Prize in Physiology or Medicine along with Crick and Wilkins in 1962 for his work on DNA, Watson wrote a book titled *The Double Helix*. It is controversial for his treatment of Rosalind.

Connection to Rosalind: Wilkins often brought him to King's lab, and Rosalind knew Watson from many conferences. They were both working on DNA. Watson used Rosalind's data, given to him by Wilkins, to build a model of DNA, which led to a Nobel Prize. Although he was friendly toward Rosalind, he failed to give her full credit for her work on DNA.

Other work: Watson moved on from Cambridge first to Caltech, then to a professorship at Harvard, and then to the Biological Lab at Cold Springs Harbor, which he headed.

Lawrence Bragg (1890–1971)

Bragg was an Australian-born British physicist and X-ray crystallographer at Cambridge's Cavendish lab.

Notable work: Lawrence Bragg was awarded the Nobel Prize in Physics, together with his father, William Henry Bragg, at the age of twenty-five, making him the youngest recipient of this prize to date. Bragg's Nobel was in recognition for the methodology of studying crystal structures by X-ray diffraction, which the Braggs had developed at the University of Leeds.

Connection to Rosalind: Watson and Crick worked for Bragg who oversaw Cavendish lab. Bragg and Randall had to talk often when the competition between Cavendish's lab and King's lab came to a critical point.

Birkbeck Lab

John D. Bernal (1901–1971)

Bernal was a pioneer in the X-ray crystallography field. His name is associated with the Bernal chart, an index of X-ray diffraction photographs of single crystals, the Bernal sphere, Bernal stacking, Bernal-Fowler rules, pepsin, vitamin D2, the sterols, TMV, and authoring over twenty-four publications.

Notable work: Bernal's PhD adviser was William Henry Bragg. His students were Dorothy Hodgkin, Max Perutz, and Alan Mackay. He worked closely with Isidor Fankuchen and won a joint prize—Cambridge University's Sudbury-Hardyman Prize—with Ronald Norrish.

Connection to Rosalind: In 1938 Bernal left Cambridge to become a physics professor at Birkbeck College where Rosalind worked for him, in his lab, from 1953–1958.

Other work: In addition to numerous awards and papers, Bernal was the president of the World Peace Council.

Aaron Klug (1926–2018)

Klug was an English biophysicist and chemist, who started work, in 1953, at Birkbeck lab with Rosalind and Bernal. Klug's name is associated with crystallography electron microscopy, RNA, zinc fingers, and neurofibrils in Alzheimer's disease, the Scripps Research Institute, the Wellcome Trust, the Wellcome Sanger Institute and, in turn, the Human Genome Project.

Notable work: He is known for his work on the structure of spherical viruses. He was awarded the 1982 Nobel Prize in Chemistry.

Connection to Rosalind: Rosalind was working at Birkbeck when he joined. They had adjoining rooms on the top floor of the old building but didn't get to know each other for months. They met on the stairs, and Klug became interested in TMV work at that time. They became close friends as well, and he was entrusted with her lab notes after her death.

Other work: In 1962 he moved to the newly built MRC in their Lab of Molecular Biology and was eventually named an Honorary Fellow at Cambridge. From 1986–1996, he was the director of that lab.

Noteworthy

Dorothy Crowfoot Hodgkin (1910–1994)

Hodgkin was an Egyptian-born British chemist. Her interest in chemistry started in childhood. Her mother, a botanist, encouraged her fascination in science and gave her a book about X-ray crystallography by William Henry Bragg for her sixteenth birthday.

Notable work: In 1946 she discovered the structure of penicillin. In 1956 she was responsible for the discovery of the structure of vitamin B12, which has the most complex structure of all vitamins. In 1962 Hodgkin received the Nobel Prize in Chemistry.

Connection to Rosalind: Hodgkin helped advance Rosalind's X-ray crystallography techniques by sharing her early work.

Jacques Mering (1904–1973)

Mering was an electrical engineer who was Lithuanian (then Russia) born and eventually naturalized French.

Notable work: Jacques Mering worked at the lab in Paris that used X-ray crystallography to study molecular structure. He trained under Marcel Mathieu, who learned X-ray crystallography from William Henry Bragg.

Connection to Rosalind: He met Rosalind in this Paris lab. Mering was responsible for training Rosalind in X-ray crystallography at the beginning of her career. They had a close and possibly romantic relationship.

Other work: He became the director of research at the Centre National de Recherche Scientifique in France.

Donald (Don) Caspar (1927–2021)

Caspar was an American structural biologist.

Notable work: Caspar is known for his work on the structure of tobacco mosaic virus, and he is credited with creating the term *structural biology*. His name is also associated with Caltech, University of Oxford, and Birkbeck College.

Connection to Rosalind: The year after he graduated from Yale, he worked under Rosalind where the two published numerous papers on viruses. They developed an increasingly close personal relationship in the years before her death.

Other work: He went on to open the Laboratory for Structural Biology at Boston Children's Hospital and was professor emeritus after Brandeis and worked at the Institute of Molecular Biophysics at Florida State.

Linus Pauling (1901–1994)

Pauling, an American chemist, biochemist, chemical engineer, and peace activist, is known for work on the nature of the chemical bond and on the secondary structure of proteins. Because of the number of advances credited to him, he was thought of as one of the most productive scientists in the 1900s.

Notable work: In addition to Pauling's work on DNA, he was also on the forefront of identifying sickle cell anemia and the uses of vitamin C. He started the Linus Pauling Institute. Pauling is the only person in history to have won two individual Nobel Prizes: the Nobel Prize in Chemistry (1954) and Nobel Peace Prize (1962).

Connection to Rosalind: Pauling competed with Watson and Crick in the DNA race from his lab in California. Because of Pauling's political activism, he was often prohibited from travel and therefore missed the opportunity to see Rosalind's groundbreaking photographs of DNA.

Rudolf Signer (1903–1990)

Signer was a Swiss biochemist based at the University of Bern. **Notable work:** Signer procured a DNA sample of far superior quality to any other available at the time. Gosling and Randall both considered Signer to be essential to the story of discovering the structure of DNA.
Connection to Rosalind: Rosalind used the DNA sample Signer created; it was called the Signer DNA Set. Maurice Wilkins obtained a sample of this set, derived from calf thymus, after Signer generously offered it to all takers at a London lecture.

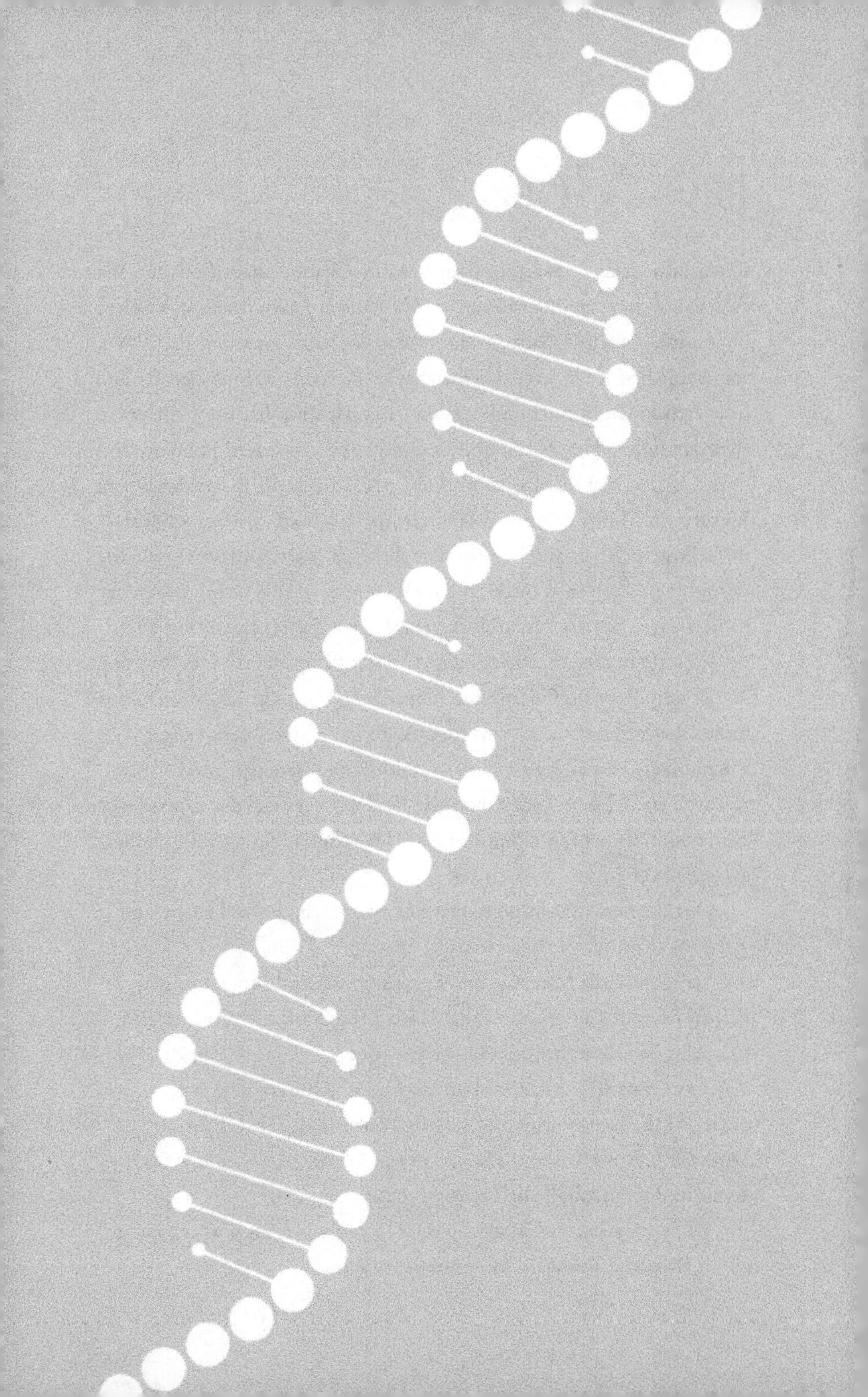

Author's Note

Rosalind's friend and confidant Anne Sayre, mortified by the disservice done to her friend in *The Double Helix*, wanted to clear her name. In 1987 Sayre's biography, *Rosalind Franklin and DNA*, was published by W. W. Norton. Sayre shared Rosalind's letters and interviewed Rosalind's colleagues, friends, and family to capture their thoughts. Her notes are exhaustive and are stored in an archive at the University of Maryland, Baltimore and kept by the American Society for Microbiology. When writing this book, we leaned heavily into those archives and believe that these primary sources enable the thoughts and feelings of the main characters in this nonfiction story to be heard. Sayre's research for the biography revealed that even a decade after her death, Rosalind had a lasting impact on her colleagues.

Rosalind's profound love for science led to three crucial discoveries in her short life of thirty-seven years. In her sixteen-year career, she published forty-five papers in prominent science journals. Her research and lab notes are exhaustive, and her personal correspondence span countless pages written by hand. These items, along with photos, are preserved in various archives.

Our deepest thanks go to the following, who helped shape and guide us through the research and writings:

To agent Erin Murphy, our shining guide and superstar, who helped us craft the proposal that landed the book with Lerner and has been our rock throughout the process.

To editors Brian Farrey-Latz and Jesseca Fusco, who truly enriched the manuscript and clarified our intent. To Editorial Director Carol Hinz and the rest of the Lerner/Zest team, who supported us through the entire process.

To Sydney Dunn-Valadez, MD, Debbie's daughter, who told her about Rosalind Franklin fourteen years ago.

To Tami Lewis Brown for her research superpowers that allowed this book to come to fruition. It would not be a book without Tami and her creative ideas, especially the Nobel Ceremony scene.

To archivist Colleen Puterbaugh of the American Society for Microbiology, who pulled box after box from the archive stacks, arrived early, stayed late, and answered all questions, big and small.

To the University of Maryland, Baltimore for housing the Anne Sayre Collection of Rosalind Franklin Materials.

To the Wellcome Trust, the London Science Museum, and Wellcome Collection for sharing the Rosalind Franklin Papers archives and for preserving the wall Picasso drew his mural on during the World Peace Conference, a scene in this book.

To book coach Carolyn Malloy, who coached us through an early draft and gave us invaluable advice.

To Emilien Rabin for helping with French to English translations when needed.

To Kate Wadsley for her stellar photography.

And huge thanks to David and Jeff, who supported our time away as we wrote and revised.

Glossary

alkali: a base that dissolves in water to give hydroxide ions

anode: a positive electrode

bacteriophage: a virus that is parasitic within a bacterium. Most phages infect, quickly multiply within, and destroy their host cells. Also called phage.

bacterium: a single cell that lacks a distinct nuclear membrane and has a cell wall of a unique composition; plural, bacteria

chromatography: a technique for analyzing or separating mixtures of gases, liquids, or dissolved substances

cobalt therapy: a medical treatment that uses radioactive cobalt-60 to kill cancerous cells in a precise way to limit damage to nearby healthy tissues

crystalline: having the regular internal arrangement of atoms, ions, or molecules characteristic of crystals

cytoplasm: the material surrounding the nucleus of a cell. If dense, it is concerned primarily with cell movement. If less dense, it contains most of the cell's structures.

deoxyribonucleic acid (DNA): the genetic material of most living organisms. It plays a central role in the determination of hereditary characteristics.

electron microscope: a microscope that uses a beam of electrons instead of a beam of light

helical structure: something spiral in form

helix: an object having a three-dimensional shape like that of a wire uniformly in a single layer around a cylinder or cone, as in a corkscrew or spiral staircase

Hilger X-ray tube: the best quality for X-ray diffraction

ion: an atom or group of atoms that has either lost one or more electrons, making it positively charged (a cation) or gained one or more electrons, making it negatively charged (an anion). Atoms or molecules with a net electric charge due to the loss or gain of electrons.

molecular biology: the study of the structures and functions in living organisms, specifically the proteins and nucleic acids, RNA and DNA

molecule: a fundamental unit forming a chemical compound that can take part in a chemical reaction. In most covalent compounds, molecules consist of groups of atoms held together by covalent or coordinate bonds.

nucleic acid: a complex organic compound living in cells that consist of a chain of nucleotides. There are two types: DNA and RNA.

nucleotide: an organic compound consisting of a nitrogen-containing purine or pyrimidine base linked to a sugar (ribose or deoxyribose) and a phosphate group

phase: a description of the stage that a periodic motion has reached. A homogeneous part of a heterogeneous system that is separated from other parts by a distinguishable boundary. A mixture of ice and water is a two-phase system.

phosphate group: a phosphorous atom bound to four oxygen atoms but has many important roles. Along with sugars and bases, it makes up nucleic acids, such as DNA and RNA.

phosphates: salts based formally on phosphorus oxoacids and, in particular, salts of phosphoric acid

poliovirus: a highly infectious virus that targets motor neurons in the spinal cord and brain stem causing poliomyelitis, or polio. Poliomyelitis can lead to spinal and respiratory paralysis and, sometimes, death.

protein: a large group of organic compounds found in all living organisms. Proteins comprise carbon, hydrogen, oxygen, and nitrogen, and most also contain sulfur. Protein molecules consist of one or several long chains of amino acids linked in a characteristic sequence.

reflecting microscope: a microscope that uses mirrors to direct light, rather than lenses

ribonucleic acid (RNA): a nucleic acid present in all living cells. Its principal role is to act as a messenger carrying instructions from DNA and in some viruses RNA rather than DNA.

Salk vaccine: the first successful vaccine against polio was created by Dr. Jonas Salk. This vaccine is also known as the inactivated poliovirus vaccine (IPV) because it is derived from inactivated or "killed" virus. Salk created this and tested his experimental vaccine on himself and his family first before introducing it to over a million children with incredible success.

spectra: a range of electromagnetic energies arrayed in order of increasing or decreasing wavelength or frequency

spectroscopy: the study of methods of producing and analyzing spectra. The interpretations of the spectra can be used for chemical analysis for examining atomic and molecular structures.

thymus: a lymphoid organ in the neck of vertebrates, which produces T-lymphocytes for the immune system

virus: a particle that is too small to be seen with a light microscope but is capable of independent metabolism and reproduction within a living cell

X-ray: used medically and industrially to examine internal structures. X-rays can pass through many forms of matter.

X-ray crystallography: directs a beam of X-rays at a crystalline sample and records the diffraction X-rays on a photographic plate. It is used to determine the structure of crystals or molecules, such as nucleic acids.

X-ray diffraction: the diffraction of X-rays by a crystal

X-ray tube: a device for generating X-rays by accelerating electrons to a high energy electrostatic field and making them strike a metal target either in a tube containing a low-pressure gas or, as in modern tubes, in a high vacuum

Note: *Definitions are from the Oxford Science Dictionary, the World Health Organization, and Sydney Dunn-Valadez, MD.*

Source Notes

10 "To do any . . . in one's subject.": Rosalind Franklin, quoted in Jenifer Glynn, *My Sister Rosalind Franklin* (Oxford University Press, 2012), Kindle.

10 "I was told . . . was too literal-minded.": Rosalind Franklin, quoted in Brenda Maddox, *Rosalind Franklin: The Dark Lady of DNA* (Harper Perennial, 2013), Kindle.

11 "frugal rich": Maddox.

11 "very, very public-spirited family.": Maddox.

12 "We went with . . . have ever seen.": Franklin, quoted in Glynn, *My Sister Rosalind Franklin.*

12 "It is always . . . of another country.": Franklin, quoted in Glynn.

13 "stormy": Maddox, *Rosalind Franklin.*

13 "These storms were . . . too easily provoked.": Muriel Franklin, quoted in Anne Sayre, *Rosalind Franklin and DNA* (W. W. Norton, 1975), 26.

13 "Rosalind is alarmingly . . . her sums right.": Mamie Bentwich, quoted in Maddox, *Rosalind Franklin.*

14 "It makes me . . . all squidgy inside": Rosalind Franklin, quoted in Glynn, *My Sister Rosalind Franklin.*

14 "But don't tell . . . not supposed to": Franklin, quoted in Glynn.

15 "They would have . . . of the family": Weill, Paris. complete notes from interviews with P. Hemily, V. and D. Luzzati, J. Mering and R. Glassner and A. Weill, n.d., Box 4, Folder 21, Anne Sayre Collection of Rosalind Franklin Materials, Center for the History of Microbiology ASM Archives, University of Maryland at Baltimore College.

15 "You look at . . . explanation for life.": Franklin, quoted in Maddox, *Rosalind Franklin.*

17 "geometrical basis for inheritance": Franklin, quoted in Maddox.

17 "Nobody here seems . . . on in Germany": Franklin, quoted in Glynn, *My Sister Rosalind Franklin.*

17 "This evening there . . . in evening dress.": Franklin, quoted in Maddox, *Rosalind Franklin.*

17 "It is surprisingly . . . is empty then.": Franklin, quoted in Glynn, *My Sister Rosalind Franklin.*

17 "I couldn't bear to have them bombed.": Franklin to family, quoted in Glynn.

19 "he became most . . . —in fact, several.": Franklin, quoted in Maddox, *Rosalind Franklin.*

19 "stupid, bigoted, deceitful, ill-mannered and tyrannical.": Franklin, quoted in Maddox.

21 "If ever you . . . let me know.": Franklin to Weill, quoted in Maddox.

22 "I love the . . . and the food.": Franklin, quoted in Maddox.

23 "When she arrived . . . 'unEnglished'": D. D. Lawrence, quoted in Maddox.

23 "Labo": Howard Markel, *The Secret of Life: Rosalind Franklin, James Watson, Francis Crick, and the Discovery of DNA's Double Helix* (W. W. Norton, 2021), Kindle.

23 "I shall be very sorry to leave here.": Franklin, quoted in Glynn, *My Sister Rosalind Franklin.*

24 "a fresh thrill every day.": Franklin, quoted in Glynn.

24 "Though my circle . . . I work with.": Franklin, quoted in Maddox, *Rosalind Franklin.*

25 "Freedom is the . . . have found it.": Franklin, quoted in Glynn, *My Sister Rosalind Franklin.*

25 "I went last . . . crowd of 30,000.": Franklin, quoted in Glynn.

26 "it was so . . . to be funny.": Franklin, quoted in Glynn.

26 "by reminding him . . . in May.": Franklin, quoted in Glynn.

26 "I would willingly . . . preserve my freedom.": Franklin, quoted in Glynn.

26 "far more important . . . more frequent baths.": Franklin, quoted in Maddox, *Rosalind Franklin.*

26 "wonderful moment when . . . early morning pink.": Franklin, quoted in Glynn, *My Sister Rosalind Franklin*.

26 "I would write . . . heaven knows what.": Franklin, quoted in Glynn.

26–27 "Saturday I spent . . . again tasting wines.": Franklin, quoted in Glynn.

28 "a scruffy period . . . went to Paris.": Piper, Anne, notes, n.d., Box 4, Folder 25, Anne Sayre Collection of Rosalind Franklin Materials.

28 "with Rosalind it . . . attached to it.": Denise Luzatti, Paris, complete notes from interviews. with P. Hemily, V. and D. Luzzati, J. Mering and R. Glassner, and A. Weill, n.d., Box 4, Folder 21, Anne Sayre Collection of Rosalind Franklin Materials.

28 "tragic.": Maddox, *Rosalind Franklin*.

29 "felt sure she . . . these were transgressed.": Jacques Mering, Paris, Anne Sayre Collection of Rosalind Franklin Materials.

29 "Rosalind could be . . . who made mistakes.": Margaret North, interview, May 15, 1970, correspondence, n.d., Box 4, Folder 19, Anne Sayre Collection of Rosalind Franklin Materials.

29 "Rosalind couldn't have . . . but absolutely superior.'": Mrs. Simon Altmann, notes from interview, n.d., Box 2, Folder 2, Anne Sayre Collection of Rosalind Franklin Materials.

29 "There was in . . . to be liked.": Vittorio Luzzati, Luzzati, Vittorio and Denise, notes from interview, n.d., Box 4, Folder 13, Anne Sayre Collection of Rosalind Franklin Materials.

29 "made it impossible . . . part of this.": Mering, Paris, complete notes from interviews with P. Hemily, V. and D. Luzzati, J. Mering and R. Glassner, and A. Weill, n.d., Box 4, Folder 21, Anne Sayre Collection of Rosalind Franklin Materials.

29 "who courted Rosalind . . . see this either.": Mering, Paris,

Anne Sayre Collection of Rosalind Franklin Materials.

29–30 “she didn’t condemn . . . were true ones.”: Denise Luzzati, Paris, Anne Sayre Collection of Rosalind Franklin Materials.

30 “preference for Paris . . . the Parisian climate.”: Franklin, quoted in Glynn, *My Sister Rosalind Franklin*.

31 “After very careful . . . yourself and Gosling.”: John T. Randall, quoted in Markel, *The Secret of Life*.

31 “I am, of . . . all things biological.”: Randall, quoted in Maddox, *Rosalind Franklin*.

32 “invisible factors.”: C. N. El-Hani, “Mendel in Genetics Teaching: Some Contributions from History of Science and Articles for Teachers,” *Science & Education* 24 (2015): 173–201, https://doi.org/10.1007/s11191-014-9685-y.

36 “I knew she . . . and related substances.”: “Papers of M H F Wilkins: Draft Text Relating to Maurice Wilkins’s Work at St Andrews University, and to Rosalind Franklin,” K/PP178/6/4/2, n.d., Wellcome Collection, https://wellcomelibrary.org/item/b20051256.

37 “What is it . . . dreary by comparison.”: Rosalind Franklin to Anne Sayre, March 3, 1952, Franklin, Rosalind E.—correspondence to her family, F. H. C. Crick, M. Mathieu, A. L. Patterson, A. and D. Sayre, A. Weill, n.d., Box 3, Folder 1, Anne Sayre Collection of Rosalind Franklin Materials.

38 “I still spend . . . here [in Paris].”: Franklin, quoted in Glynn, *My Sister Rosalind Franklin*.

38 “I was formally . . . my day-to-day supervisor.”: Gosling, quoted in “Raymond Gosling on the DNA Race,” Cold Spring Harbor Laboratory, accessed June 20, 2023, http://library.cshl.edu/oralhistory/interview/james-d-watson/discovering-double-helix/race-double-helix/.

40 “It was my . . . was getting nowhere.”: Gosling, quoted in “Raymond Gosling.”

40–41 “I had a . . . say, is history.”: Gosling, quoted in “Raymond Gosling.”

41 “Eureka”: Gosling, quoted in “Raymond Gosling.”

43 “inflammable air.”: Henry Cavendish, quoted in “Hydrogen,” ACS Chemistry for Life, last modified June 22, 2020, https://www.acs.org/molecule-of-the-week/archive/h/hydrogen.html.

44 “the sample’s water . . . a salt solution”: Markel, *The Secret of Life.*

44 “Rosalind would say . . . say so, bing!”: Gosling, Raymond G., interview, n.d., Box 4, Folder 2, Anne Sayre Collection of Rosalind Franklin Materials.

44–45 “she had been . . . assistant.”: James D. Watson, *The Double Helix: A Personal Account of the Discovery of the Structure of DNA* (Scribner, 2011), Kindle.

45 “She’s pushy and . . . another person’s lab.”: Watson.

45 “she was an independent . . . no way subject to Wilkins”: Watson.

45 “You’re completely wrong.”: Franklin, quoted in Gosling, Raymond G., interview, Box 4, Anne Sayre Collection of Rosalind Franklin Materials.

45 “Rosy’s Parlour”: Maddox, *Rosalind Franklin.*

45 “little schoolboys”: Franklin, quoted in Maddox.

45 “It’s known as . . . than a lab.”: Gosling, Raymond G., interview, May 18, 1970, Box 4, Folder 2, Anne Sayre Collection of Rosalind Franklin Materials.

47 “To let sexist . . . consequences were serious.”: “Papers of M H F Wilkins: Draft Text Concerning Wilkins’s Reaction to Accusations of Sexism Towards Rosalind Franklin, with Related Papers,” Wellcome Collection, accessed June 21, 2025, https://wellcomelibrary.org/item/b20051360.

48 “Communist”: Maddox, *Rosalind Franklin.*

48 “Her family doesn’t . . . for my family.”: Brown, Geoffrey, notes from interview, n.d., Box 2, Folder 3, Anne Sayre Collection of Rosalind Franklin Materials.

48 “She wears a . . . looks quite lovely.”: Gosling, quoted in “Raymond Gosling.”

48 "[serving] marvelous French . . . so gracefully done.": Mrs. Simon Altmann, notes from interview, n.d., Box 2, Folder 2, Anne Sayre Collection of Rosalind Franklin Materials.

48 "Rosalind puts a . . . nice for people": Mrs. Simon Altmann, notes from interview.

50 "pile of pennies.": Astbury, quoted in Robert C. Olby, *The Path to the Double Helix. The Discovery of DNA* (Dover, 1994), Kindle.

51 "I noticed you . . . have helped you.": John Randall to Wilkins, June 5, 1951, John Randall's correspondence as director, biophysics unit, "Papers of M H F Wilkins," K/PP178/3/35/3, Wellcome Collection, https://wellcomecollection.org/works/m5shvnh5.

52 "quite scary": Markel, *The Secret of Life.*

52 "little Jewish girl": Watson, quoted in Markel.

52 "Crick in a . . . of his gums.": Maddox, *Rosalind Franklin.*

53 "Jim [Watson] and . . . both of us.": Francis Crick, *What Mad Pursuit: A Personal View of Scientific Discovery* (Basic Books, 1988), Kindle.

54 "It seemed that . . . into a helix.": Maurice Wilkins, *The Third Man of the Double Helix: The Autobiography of Maurice Wilkins* (Oxford University Press, 2003), Kindle.

54 "discernable central 'X' or a 'crossways'": Markel, *The Secret of Life.*

55 "Go back to your microscopes!": Franklin, quoted in Wilkins, *The Third Man.*

56 "Because her own . . . triflers of science.": Sayre, *Rosalind Franklin and DNA*, 37.

57 "Until Rosalind got . . . a two-phase structure": Gosling, Raymond G., interview, May 18, 1970, Box 4, Folder 2, Anne Sayre Collection of Rosalind Franklin Materials.

59 "base-pairings.": Wilkins, *The Third Man.*

60 "How dare you . . . data for me!": Wilkins.

60 "Her air of . . . feeling of panic.": Wilkins.

60 "If you believed . . . simply shut up.": Gosling, Raymond G., interview, May 18, 1970, Box 4, Folder 2,

Anne Sayre Collection of Rosalind Franklin Materials.

60 "I came back . . . will have me.": Maddox, *Rosalind Franklin.*

61 "His manner of . . . a naughty child.": Wilkins, *The Third Man.*

61 "taking her out . . . liked the girl.": "Papers of M H F Wilkins: Draft Text Concerning Sexism."

61 "Wilkins was fiercely . . . disliked weak men.": Vittorio Luzzati, Paris, complete notes from interviews. with P. Hemily, V. and D. Luzzati, J. Mering and R. Glassner, and A. Weill, n.d., Box 4, Folder 21, Anne Sayre Collection of Rosalind Franklin Materials.

61 "Rosalind was attractive . . . people at King's.": Gosling, Raymond G., interview, May 18, 1970, Box 4, Folder 2, Anne Sayre Collection of Rosalind Franklin Materials.

61 "All the students . . . for their animosity.": North, Margaret, correspondence, n.d., Box 4, Folder 19, Anne Sayre Collection of Rosalind Franklin Materials.

64 "All of us . . . love with her.": Crick to Sayre, correspondence, miscellaneous, n.d., Box 2, Folder 9, Anne Sayre Collection of Rosalind Franklin Materials.

64 "She was sprawled . . . smudged lab coat": Wilkins, quoted in Markel, *The Secret of Life.*

64 "body odor": Wilkins, quoted in Markel.

64 "objected to the . . . present smelly state.": Wilkins, quoted in Markel.

66 "Rosy did not . . . the helical theory.": Watson, *Double Helix*; Markel, *The Secret of Life.*

68 "She had a . . . the honesty won.": Sayre, *Rosalind Franklin and DNA*, 37.

68 "You're wrong.": Markel, *The Secret of Life.*

68–69 "might make it . . . within the week.": Watson, *Double Helix.*

69 "did not like . . . race with Cambridge": Wilkins, *The Third Man.*

70 "produced the theory . . . sheet of paper": Markel, *The Secret of Life.*

71 “kingpin.”: Watson, *Double Helix*.

72 “2, 3 or . . . per helical unit”: Sayre, *Rosalind Franklin and DNA*, 126.

72 “The idea of . . . a last resort.”: Watson, *Double Helix*.

72 “We made asses of ourselves.”: Crick, quoted in “The Race for the Double Helix,” BBC Internet Archive, accessed June 20, 2023, https://archive.org/details/TheRacefortheDoubleHelix.

73 “I knew that . . . and influence people.”: Gosling, Raymond G., interview, n.d., Box 4, Folder 2, Anne Sayre Collection of Rosalind Franklin Materials.

74 “Rosalind didn’t like . . . the unique solution?”: Gosling, Raymond G., interview, May 18, 1970, Box 4, Folder 2, Anne Sayre Collection of Rosalind Franklin Materials.

75 “She developed a . . . sometimes proved extreme.”: Sayre, *Rosalind Franklin and DNA*, 40.

76 “We ought to . . . need for collaboration.”: Wilkins, *The Third Man*.

76 “The middle and . . . but distinctly boring.”: Franklin, Rosalind E.—correspondence to her family, F. H. C. Crick, M. Mathieu, A. L. Patterson, A. and D. Sayre, A. Weill, n.d., Box 3, Folder 1, Anne Sayre Collection of Rosalind Franklin Materials.

78 “It’s what a crystallographer would do”: Luzzati, quoted in Markel, *The Secret of Life*.

79 “I suspect that . . . am in England.”: Franklin to Sayre, March 3, 1952, Franklin, Rosalind E.—correspondence to her family, F. H. C. Crick, M. Mathieu, A. L. Patterson, A. and D. Sayre, and A. Weill, n.d., Box 3, Folder 1, Anne Sayre Collection of Rosalind Franklin Materials.

80 “were the best . . . But Rosalind!”: Dorothy Hodgkin, quoted in Markel, *The Secret of Life*.

80 “a good brain among them”: Markel.

80–81 “Rosalind’s unhappiness at . . . its highest degree.”: Paris, complete notes from interviews. with P. Hemily, V. and D. Luzzati, J. Mering and R. Glassner, and A. Weill, n.d., Box 4, Folder 21, Anne Sayre Collection of Rosalind Franklin Materials.

81 "King's had neither foreigners nor Jews.": Franklin, quoted in Markel, *The Secret of Life.*

82 "fly over as . . . was justifiable homicide.": Sayre, quoted in Maddox, *Rosalind Franklin.*

83 "she had discovered . . . in professional terms.": Sayre, *Rosalind Franklin and DNA*, 45.

83 "visited by a . . . from another planet.": Maddox, *Rosalind Franklin.*

84 "One of the . . . some male agent.": Brown, Geoffrey, notes from interview, n.d., Box 2, Folder 3, Anne Sayre Collection of Rosalind Franklin Materials.

84 "might be possible . . . of the crystal": Maddox, *Rosalind Franklin.*

86 "I'm afraid we . . . attitude towards her.": Crick, quoted in Maddox.

88 "She could stick . . . have been betrayal.": Sayre, *Rosalind Franklin and DNA*, 38.

89 "There was quite . . . on the floor": Gosling, quoted in Maddox, *Rosalind Franklin.*

89 "And it was great fun!": Gosling, quoted in "Raymond Gosling."

89 "She could be . . . to work with.": Gosling, quoted in "Raymond Gosling."

90 "He will take . . . I get back.": Franklin, quoted in Sayre, *Rosalind Franklin and DNA*, 140.

90 "two pitchmen in . . . of a helix.": Erwin Chargaff, quoted in Maddox, *Rosalind Franklin.*

91 "The situation [at King's] was impossible.": Randall, John, notes from interview, n.d., Box 4, Folder 27, Anne Sayre Collection of Rosalind Franklin Materials.

92 "lop-sided.": Wilkins, *The Third Man.*

92 "death of the helix.": Satirical note announcing the death of the DNA helix—Digital Collections—National Library of Medicine, accessed June 25, 2025, https://collections.nlm.nih.gov/catalog/nlm:nlmuid-101584582X360-doc.

93 “recent indications seemed . . . point towards helices.”: Wilkins, *The Third Man*.

94 “Often overlooked is . . . anything but helical.”: Gosling, quoted in Markel, *The Secret of Life*; Maddox, *Rosalind Franklin*.

95 “The phrase ‘war . . . condemned sexist rubbish.”: “Papers of M H F Wilkins: Draft Text Concerning Sexism.”

96 “indication of a helix.”: Franklin, quoted in Sayre, *Rosalind Franklin and DNA*, 146–147.

96 “sharper, but very complex.”: Franklin, quoted in Sayre, 146–147.

97 “Phage genetics have . . . are rather fast”: Wilkins, quoted in Crick, *What Mad Pursuit*.

102 “The genetic master . . . proteins, was DNA.”: Pauling, quoted in Thomas Hager, *Force of Nature: The Life of Linus Pauling* (Monroe, 2011), Kindle.

103 “indication that either . . . a serious threat.”: Hager.

104 “wunderkind”: Markel, *The Secret of Life*.

104–105 “Franklin barks often . . . last saw you.”: Markel.

106 “Everyone who touched . . . you go mad.”: Wilkins, *The Third Man*.

106 “Fourier transforms of . . . on a helix.”: W. Cochran et al., “The Structure of Synthetic Polypeptides. I. The Transform of Atoms on a Helix,” *Acta Crystallographica* 5 (September 10, 1952): 581–586, https://doi.org/10.1107/S0365110X52001635.

107 “Ever considered whether . . . around one another.”: Crick, quoted in Hager, *Force of Nature*; Markel, *The Secret of Life*.

107 “coiled coils.”: F. H. C. Crick, “Is α-Keratin a Coiled Coil?,” *Nature* 170 (November 22, 1952): 882–883, https://doi.org/10.1038/170882b0.

108 “This [coiled coil] . . . alone did not.”: Pauling. quoted in Hager, *Force of Nature*.

108 “Helices were in . . . along helical lines.”: Crick, *What Mad Pursuit*.

108 "... coiled coils": Linus Pauling and Robert B. Corey, "Compound Helical Configurations of Polypeptide Chains: Structure of Proteins of the α-Keratin Type," *Nature* 171 (January 10, 1953): 59–61, https://doi.org/10.1038/171059a0.

109 "I exploded: for ... over the years.": Wilkins, *The Third Man.*

109 "Rosalind seemed so ... her for anything.": Wilkins.

109 "I've decided to ... her non-helical DNA.": Wilkins.

109 "Rather than build ... about his neck.": Watson, *Double Helix.*

110 "The fact that ... the DNA pattern.": Watson.

110 "No more dividends ... not through TMV.": Watson, quoted in Markel, *The Secret of Life.*

111 "the value of ... a devil's advocate": Raymond Gosling et al., "Seven Ages of the PhD," *Nature* 472 (April 20, 2011): 283, https://doi.org/10.1038/472283a.

111 "I always thought ... matter of time.": Pauling, quoted in Hager, *Force of Nature.*

111 "Perhaps we have a triple-chain structure!": Pauling, quoted in Hager.

111–112 "a question of ... in some way.": Pauling, quoted in Hager.

112 "We have, we ... a beautiful one.": Pauling, quoted in Hager.

112 "extraordinarily tightly-packed model": Markel, *The Secret of Life.*

113 "Dear Randall: I ... yours, Linus Pauling": Linus Pauling, letter to Randall, December 31, 1952, Special Collections and Archives Research Center, OSU Libraries, Oregon State University, https://scarc.library.oregonstate.edu/coll/pauling/calendar/1952/12/31.html.

113 "We have formulated ... helical polynucleotide chains.": Linus Pauling and Robert B. Corey, "A Proposed Structure for the Nucleic Acids," *PNAS* 39, no. 2 (February 1, 1953): 84–97, https://doi.org/10.1073/pnas.39.2.84.

114 “I explained how . . . the Nobel Prize.”: Watson, *Double Helix*.

114 “I had recently . . . at Birkbeck College.”: Wilkins, *The Third Man*.

115 “Let’s have some . . . of our eyes.”: Wilkins, quoted in Markel, *The Secret of Life*.

115–116 “One day in . . . keep the photograph!”: Wilkins.

116 “more clearly than ever before.”: Wilkins.

116 “exceptionally long, and . . . structure of A-DNA.”: Wilkins.

116 “suggested that the . . . and figure-of-eight shapes.”: Markel, *The Secret of Life*.

117 “I was taken . . . might believe that.”: Wilkins, *The Third Man*.

117 “Why did she not show it?”: Wilkins.

117 “Rosie’s colloquium made . . . simple as that.”: Wilkins.

119 “They were mucking . . . have done it.”: Crick, Francis H. C., notes from interview, n.d., Box 2, Folder 9, Anne Sayre Collection of Rosalind Franklin Materials.

120 “beginning the DNA . . . think about it.”: Wilkins, *The Third Man*.

121 “made a similar lunge toward him”: Watson, *Double Helix*.

122 “What is the pattern like?”: Watson.

122 “Maurice [Wilkins] went . . . the ‘B’ structure”: Watson.

122 “My mouth fell . . . began to race”: Watson.

124 “Do you have . . . each other’s shoulders.’”: Gosling, quoted in Naomi Attar, “Raymond Gosling: The Man Who Crystallized Genes,” *Genome Biology* 24, no. 93 (2023): 1–12, https://doi.org/10.1186/s13059-023-02946-5.

125 “was completely different . . . nonsense.”: Watson, *Double Helix*.

125 “all the hydrogen . . . identical in shape.”: Watson.

126 “The hydrogen-bonding requirement . . . only with cytosine.”: Watson.

126 “We needed a . . . Rosalind Franklin’s data.”: Crick, quoted in Markel, *The Secret of Life*.

126 "subsequently admitted to . . . secret of life.": Watson, *Double Helix*.

126–127 "If we deserve . . . sorts of DNA.": Crick, *What Mad Pursuit*.

127 "until exact coordinates . . . all the atoms.": Watson, *Double Helix*.

127 "I intend to . . . on model building.": Wilkins, quoted in Watson.

127 "Our dark lady . . . in our hands.": Wilkins, quoted in Markel, *The Secret of Life*.

127 "very strongly characteristic . . . a helical structure.": Franklin, quoted in Aaron Klug, "Rosalind Franklin and the Discovery of the Structure of DNA," *Nature* 219 (August 24, 1968): 810, https://www.nature.com/articles/219808a0.

128 "not receive a . . . work out himself.": Watson, *Double Helix*.

128 "There was not . . . benefit to biology.": Watson.

129 "With obvious pleasure, . . . a misguided feminist.": Watson.

129 "I had feared . . . conversation between equals.": Watson.

130–131 "we wish to . . . considerable biological interest": Watson.

131 "Nevertheless, since the . . . may be altered.": Rosalind E. Franklin and R. G. Gosling. "The Structure of Sodium Thymonucleate Fibres. II. The Cylindrically Symmetrical Patterson Function," *Acta Crystallographica* 6, no. 8–9 (September 10, 1953): 678–685, https://doi.org/10.1107/S0365110X53001940.

131 "You were always . . . nothing of it.": Odile Crick, quoted in Crick, *What Mad Pursuit*.

132 "only justice": John Randall, correspondence, n.d., Box 4, Folder 27, Anne Sayre Collection of Rosalind Franklin Materials.

132 "It seemed almost . . . see, so beautiful!": Watson, quoted in Edward Edelson, *Francis Crick and James Watson and the Building Blocks of Life* (Oxford University Press, 1998), Kindle.

132 "what she touched, she adorned.": Klug, quoted in Sayre, *Rosalind Franklin and DNA*, 214.

136 “The intensity was . . . met her recognized.”: Sayre, 26–27.

136 “a big enough . . . people [their] independence.”: Caraffi, A.J., notes, n.d., Box 2, Folder 4, Anne Sayre Collection of Rosalind Franklin Materials.

137–138 “I shall be . . . all the same”: Franklin to Adrienne Weill, March 2, 1946, Franklin, Rosalind E.—correspondence to her family, F. H. C. Crick, M. Mathieu, A. L. Patterson, A. and D. Sayre, A. Weill, n.d., Box 3, Folder 1, Anne Sayre Collection of Rosalind Franklin Materials.

139 “Rosalind had beakers . . . catch the drips”: Kranjc, Katarina, correspondence, n.d., Box 4, Folder 11, Anne Sayre Collection of Rosalind Franklin Materials.

139 “No, I’ll do . . . on the wall.”: Andrew P. Brown, “JD Bernal: The Sage of Science,” *Journal of Physics: Conference Series* 57, no. 1 (June 1, 2006): 61–72, https://iopscience.iop.org/article/10.1088/1742-6596/57/1/006.

141 “contagium vivum fluidum.”: Martinus Willem Beijerinck, “Concerning a Contagium Vivum Fluidum as a Cause of the Spot-Disease of Tobacco Leaves,” *Phytopathological Classics*, no. 7 (1942): 33, https://www.apsnet.org/edcenter/apsnetfeatures/Documents/1998/BeijerckSpotDiseaseTobaccoLeaves.PDF.

141 “needle-like crystals”: “Tobacco Mosaic Virus: Pioneering Research for a Century,” *Philosophical Transactions: Biological Sciences* 354, no. 1383 (March 29, 1999): 521–529, https://www.jstor.org/stable/i203455.

143 “Rosalind believes that . . . borrow or buy”: Bernal, quoted in “The Papers of Rosalind Franklin: Franklin File Kept by Professor Bernal, Birkbeck College,” FRNK 2/31, Wellcome Collection, accessed June 21, 2025, https://wellcomecollection.org/works/wtkxmddq.

143 “Deeply indebted to Dr. R.E. Franklin.”: Raymond Gosling, “X-ray Diffraction Studies of Deoxyribose Nucleic Acid,” King’s College London, 1954, https://archives.kingscollections.org/index.php/kdbp-5-1.

144 "gravitas, demeanor, and . . . a great scientist.": Maddox, *Rosalind Franklin.*

144 "Facts are facts, Francis.": Franklin, quoted in Maddox.

144 "I'm sorry you . . . which Watson used.": "The Papers of Rosalind Franklin: Correspondence Regarding Franklin's Research," FRNK 2/33, Wellcome Collection, accessed June 21, 2025, https://wellcomecollection.org/works/xx7gee23.

145 "RNA sensitive . . . easily damaged.": "The Papers of Rosalind Franklin: Correspondence Regarding Franklin's Research."

146 "I gradually became . . . the virus work.": Klug, quoted in "The Papers of Rosalind Franklin: Professor Bernal and Virus Research at Birkbeck College," FRNK 2/37, Wellcome Collection, accessed June 21, 2025, https://wellcomecollection.org/works/a7rcdzyk.

146 "She noticed. . . . She noticed everything.": Klug, quoted in Sayre, *Rosalind Franklin and DNA*, 157.

146 "Her single-mindedness made . . . a first-class experimentalist.": Klug, quoted in Maddox, *Rosalind Franklin.*

147 "Her choice was . . . was also joyful.": Sayre, *Rosalind Franklin and DNA*, 26–27.

148 "study of structures of plant viruses.": Kenneth C. Holmes, *Aaron Klug—A Long Way from Durban: A Biography* (Cambridge University Press, 2017), 82, Kindle.

150 "Jim [Watson] and . . . ever, Francis [Crick]": Crick, quoted in Maddox, *Rosalind Franklin.*

151 "gainfully employed in . . . with American labor.": Maddox.

151 "There is an . . . much of it.": Franklin, quoted in Maddox.

151 "Meals are enormous, . . . said 'hot dogs.'": Franklin, quoted in Maddox.

152 "having the bemused . . . an English poet.": Maddox.

152 "The sky-scraper group . . . like mountain scenery.": Franklin, quoted in Maddox.

152 "America is really . . . across in England.": Franklin, quoted in Maddox.

152 "I looked in . . . a white horse": Franklin, quoted in Maddox.

152–153 "The front door . . . red tile roofs.": Franklin, quoted in Maddox.

153 "[Americans are] kind . . . I've met anywhere.": Franklin, quoted in Maddox.

153 "four honorary members . . . each amino acid.": Watson, quoted in Angela N. H. Creager and Gregory J. Morgan, "After the Double Helix: Rosalind Franklin's Research on Tobacco Mosaic Virus," *Isis* 99, no. 2 (June 2008): 239–272, https://www.journals.uchicago.edu/doi/10.1086/588626.

153 "Watson and I . . . and their coworkers.": Crick, quoted in Maddox, *Rosalind Franklin.*

154–155 "Only those who . . . all are different.": Pirie to Franklin, December 6, 1954, "The Papers of Rosalind Franklin: Correspondence Regarding Franklin's Research," FRNK 2/33, Wellcome Collection, https://wellcomecollection.org/works/xx7gee23.

155 "Dear Dr. Pirie, . . . sincerely, Rosalind Franklin": Franklin to Pirie, "The Papers of Rosalind Franklin: Correspondence."

155 "structurally equivalent.": Franklin to Pirie, "The Papers of Rosalind Franklin: Correspondence."

156 "I regret to . . . any virus solution.": Franklin to Siegel, "The Papers of Rosalind Franklin: Correspondence."

157 "significant differences between . . . common TMV strain.": "The Papers of Rosalind Franklin: Correspondence."

158 "The [my] position, there . . . get, if any.": Franklin, quoted in Glynn, *My Sister Rosalind*, 88.

158 "What's new?": "The Papers of Rosalind Franklin: Professor Bernal and Virus Research at Birkbeck College," Wellcome Collection.

159–160 “[Slater] appears to . . . a London university.”: Franklin, quoted in “The Papers of Rosalind Franklin: Papers Relating to the Agricultural Research Council’s Research Group on TMV,” FRNK 2/36, Wellcome Collection, accessed June 21, 2025, 14, https://wellcomecollection.org/works/k7ug2epw.

160 “The rest of . . . request [were] ignored.”: Franklin, quoted in “The Papers of Rosalind Franklin: Papers Relating to the Agricultural Research Council’s Research Group,” 14.

161 “It’s because the . . . woman directing it.”: Franklin, quoted in Sayre, *Rosalind Franklin and DNA*, 177.

161 “He told me . . . Principal Scientific Officer.”: Franklin to Slater, “The Papers of Rosalind Franklin: Papers Relating to the Agricultural Research Council’s Research Group.”

161 “similar assurance . . . I . . . in this matter.”: Franklin to Slater, “The Papers of Rosalind Franklin: Papers Relating to the Agricultural Research Council’s Research Group.”

161 “my dear”: Slater, quoted in Maddox, *Rosalind Franklin*, 263.

161 “To reach that . . . the ‘exceptionally distinguished.’”: Slater, quoted in Maddox, 263.

161–162 “The question of . . . age and experience.”: Franklin to Bernal, “The Papers of Rosalind Franklin: Papers Relating to the Agricultural Research Council’s Research Group.”

162 “an equator of the pattern”: Franklin and Holmes, quoted in Sayre, *Rosalind Franklin and DNA*, 180.

163 “more rapport with . . . of the men”: Don Caspar, quoted in Maddox, *Rosalind Franklin*.

163 “Hey, Ros”: Caspar, quoted in Maddox.

163 “Somehow the young . . . a disarming friendliness.”: Holmes, quoted in Maddox.

163 “helical groove”: Maddox.

164 “disaggregated.”: “The Papers of Rosalind Franklin: Correspondence.”

164 “stacked on top . . . form a rod.”: “The Papers of Rosalind Franklin: Correspondence.”

164 “We must remain . . . research workers overseas.”: Franklin, quoted in Maddox, *Rosalind Franklin*, 263.

165 “She insisted on being daring.”: Sayre, *Rosalind Franklin and DNA*, 185.

166 “It is not . . . strand [in TMV].”: Franklin, quoted in G. E. W. Wolstenholme, *The Nature of Viruses* (John Wiley and Sons), 53, Google Books.

166 “I would be . . . caves at Altamira.”: Franklin, quoted in Maddox, *Rosalind Franklin*, 265.

167 “But, did anyone?”: Crick, quoted in Maddox.

168 “Rosalind used to . . . spoke about Don.”: Ethel Tessman, quoted in Maddox.

168 “Most telling for . . . talked about her.”: Irwin Tessman, quoted in Maddox.

168 “She is joyful . . . delightful and generous.”: Maddox.

168 “Perhaps the most . . . along its summit.”: Franklin, quoted in Maddox.

169 “I hope I shall see you.”: Franklin, quoted in Maddox.

169 “I’m going to . . . Don after all.”: Franklin, quoted in Maddox.

169 “she might have . . . might have married.”: Maddox.

170 “We never discussed . . . other at all.”: Roland Franklin, quoted in Maddox.

170 “I wish I were.”: Rosalind Franklin, quoted in Maddox.

170 “URGENT.”: Maddox.

171 “tennis ball . . . size . . . a croquet ball.”: Livingstone, quoted in Maddox.

171 “The findings are . . . daughter has cancer.”: Livingstone, quoted in Maddox.

171 “It could only . . . store’s entire stock.”: Maddox.

171 “the finished structure . . . cylinder of cardboard.”: Holmes, *Aaron Klug—A Long Way from Durban*, 107.

172 “[I had] been . . . love with Mering.”: Franklin, quoted in Maddox, *Rosalind Franklin*.

172 “Please stop worrying . . . time next month.”: Franklin, Rosalind E.—correspondence to her family, Anne Sayre Collection of Rosalind Franklin Materials.

172 “My mother seems . . . than last time.”: Franklin, quoted in Maddox, *Rosalind Franklin*.

173 “We are now . . . carry us on!”: Franklin, Rosalind E.—correspondence to her family, Anne Sayre Collection of Rosalind Franklin Materials.

174 “We are fixed . . . kind American tax-payers.”: Franklin to Sayre, October 8, 1957, Franklin, Rosalind E.—correspondence to her family, Anne Sayre Collection of Rosalind Franklin Materials.

174 “a glorious weekend in Zermatt.”: Maddox, *Rosalind Franklin*.

175 “No one who . . . living under threat.”: Maddox, 292.

175 “looking lovely, gay and happy.”: Maddox, 292.

176 “She felt her . . . achievement being curtailed”: Sayre, *Rosalind Franklin and DNA*, 187.

176 “. . . parent’s refrigerator”: Maddox, *Rosalind Franklin*.

177 “that Rosalind, rather . . . the test tubes.”: Maddox, 295.

177 “That photo’s worth 10,000 pounds!”: Bernal, quoted in Holmes, *Aaron Klug—A Long Way from Durban*, 104.

179 “found her in . . . by her side.”: Maddox, *Rosalind Franklin*, 295.

179 “She would crawl . . . almost to tears.”: Maddox, 301.

179 “She had a very strong will.”: Luzzati, Paris, Anne Sayre Collection of Rosalind Franklin Materials.

179 “It was heartbreakingly . . . symptoms of illness.”: Sayre, Paris, Anne Sayre Collection of Rosalind Franklin Materials.

179 “I’ve known people . . . to the end.”: Sayre, *Rosalind Franklin and DNA*, 187.

180 “I still hope . . . go over together.”: Franklin, quoted in Maddox, *Rosalind Franklin*.

180 “Her hair had . . . ‘would get well.’”: Mering, Paris, complete notes from interviews. with P. Hemily, V. and

D. Luzzati, J. Mering and R. Gleasner, and A. Weill, n.d., Box 4, Folder 21, Anne Sayre Collection of Rosalind Franklin Materials.

180 "She [Rosalind] was defying death itself.": Mering.

180 "Although I am . . . next few months.": Franklin, quoted in Maddox, *Rosalind Franklin.*

180–181 "She fought death . . . I miss her.": Sayre, *Rosalind Franklin and DNA*, 187.

184 "Her work on . . . benefit to mankind.": Rosalind Franklin's grave marker at Willesden Jewish Cemetery, London, England.

184–185 "Next on her . . . would have approved.": Maddox, *Rosalind Franklin*, 297.

186 "She was very . . . by silly questions.": Alice Franklin, quoted in Maddox.

186 "Aware of our . . . had been doing.": Glynn, *My Sister Rosalind Franklin.*

186 "Rosalind Franklin's early . . . loss to science.": Bernal, quoted in Maddox, *Rosalind Franklin.*

186 "discovered the fundamental . . . carbon was made.": "Rosalind Franklin and Her Work on Virus Structures," Churchill Archives Centre, accessed June 21, 2025, https://www.chuarchivestories.uk.

187 "careful, systematic experimental . . . states of DNA.": Klug, "Rosalind Franklin and the Discovery of the Structure of DNA," 844.

188 "Nearly home.": Klug, 808.

188 "as the small . . . her bears witness.": Bernal, quoted in Maddox, *Rosalind Franklin.*

189 "Of all crimes . . . rob the grave.": Robert Frost, quoted in Sayre, *Rosalind Franklin and DNA*, 190.

190 "The long-standing rule . . . still been alive.": Watson, *Double Helix.*

190 "The DNA story . . . discreditable, even despicable.": "Papers of M H F Wilkins: Draft Text Relating to DNA Research: King's College London, 1950–1951," K/

PP178/6/5/11, Wellcome Collection, accessed June 21, 2025, https://wellcomelibrary.org/item/b20051372.

190 "[It was] such . . . escape such feelings?": "Papers of M H F Wilkins: Draft Text on the Immediate Impact of the Crick and Watson DNA Double Helix Model, 1953, with Related Manuscript Notes," K/PP178/6/5/19/1, Wellcome Collection.

190–192 "This version of . . . to Watson's grotesque.": Mering, Jacques, correspondence, n.d., Box 4, Folder 15, Anne Sayre Collection of Rosalind Franklin Materials.

191 "Rosalind did not . . . (shall we say?).": Sayre, *Rosalind Franklin and DNA*.

191 "Since Randall wished . . . Francis and me.": Watson, *Double Helix*.

191 "I had been . . . in the corridor.": Wilkins, *The Third Man*.

191 "[Rosalind] gave me . . . by outwitting me.": "Papers of M H F Wilkins: Draft Text Relating to the Progress of DNA Research, 1951–1952," K/PP178/6/5/12, Wellcome Collection, accessed June 21, 2025, https://wellcomecollection.org/works/n5m9xyv3/items?canvas=12.

192 "My method of . . . is worth attaining.": Franklin, quoted in Glynn, *My Sister Rosalind*.

194 "circus.": Gosling, quoted in Naomi Attar, "Raymond Gosling: The Man Who Crystallized Genes," *Genome Biology* 24, no. 93 (2023): 1-12, https://doi.org/10.1186/s13059-023-02946-5.

Selected Bibliography

Anne Sayre Collection of Rosalind Franklin Materials. Center for the History of Microbiology / ASM Archives.

Attar, Naomi. "Raymond Gosling: The Man Who Crystallized Genes." *Genome Biology* 24, no. 93 (2023): 1–12. https://doi.org/10.1186/s13059-023-02946-5.

Chen, Jenny J. *DNA and RNA*. Cavendish Square, 2017.

Cook-Deegan, Robert. *The Gene Wars: Science, Politics, and the Human Genome*. W. W. Norton, 1996.

"Correspondence Regarding Franklin's Research." FRNK 2/33. Accessed October 27, 2020. Wellcome Collection. https://wellcomecollection.org/works/xx7gee23.

Cramer, Patrick. "Rosalind Franklin and the Advent of Molecular Biology." *Cell* 182, no. 4 (July 29, 2020): 787–789. https://doi.org/10.1016/j.cell.2020.07.028.

Creager, Angela N. H., and Gregory J. Morgan. "After the Double Helix: Rosalind Franklin's Research on Tobacco Mosaic Virus." *Isis* 99, no. 2 (June 2008): 239–272. https://doi.org/10.1086/588626.

Crick, Francis. "Is Keratin a Coiled Coil?" *Nature* 170 (November 22, 1952): 882–883. https://doi.org/10.1038/170882b0.

Crick, Francis. *What Mad Pursuit: A Personal View of Scientific Discovery*. Basic Books, 1988. Kindle.

"The DNA Riddle: King's College, 1951–1953." The Rosalind Franklin Papers. National Library of Medicine Profiles in Science. Accessed October 27, 2020. https://profiles.nlm.nih.gov/spotlight/kr/feature/dna.

Edelson, Edward. *Francis Crick and James Watson and the Building Blocks of Life*. Oxford University Press, 1998. Kindle.

"Envisioning Viruses: Birkbeck College, London, 1953–1958." The Rosalind Franklin Papers. National Library of Medicine Profiles in Science. Accessed October 27, 2020. https://profiles.nlm.nih.gov/spotlight/kr/feature/viruses.

Franklin, Rosalind E. "Influence of the Bonding Electrons on the Scattering of X-Rays by Carbon." *Nature* 165 (January 14, 1950): 71–72. https://doi.org/10.1038/165071a0.

Franklin, Rosalind E. "Structure of Tobacco Mosaic Virus." *Nature* 175 (February 26, 1955): 379–381. https://doi.org/10.1038/175379a0.

Franklin Rosalind E., and R. G. Gosling. "Evidence for 2-Chain Helix in Crystalline Structure of Sodium Deoxyribonucleate." *Nature* 172 (July 25, 1953): 156–157. https://doi.org/10.1038/172156a0.

Franklin, Rosalind E., and R. G. Gosling, "Molecular Configuration in Sodium Thymonucleate." *Nature* 171 (April 25,1953): 740–741. https://doi.org/10.1038/171740a0.

Franklin, Rosalind E., and R. G. Gosling. "The Structure of Sodium Thymonucleate Fibres. I. The Influence of Water Content." *Acta Crystallographica* 6, no. 8–9 (1953): 673–677. https://doi.org/10.1107/S0365110X53001939.

Franklin, Rosalind E., and R. G. Gosling. "The Structure of Sodium Thymonucleate Fibres. II. The Cylindrically Symmetrical Patterson Function." *Acta Crystallographica* 6, no. 8–9 (September 10, 1953): 678–685. https://doi.org/10.1107/S0365110X53001940.

"Franklin File Kept by Professor Bernal, Birkbeck College." FRNK 2/31. Accessed October 27, 2020. Wellcome Collection. https://wellcomecollection.org/works/wtkxmddq.

"Franklin's Published Works." FRNK 4/1. Accessed October 27, 2020. Welcome Collection. https://wellcomecollection.org/works/u3yjkdeh.

Glynn, Jenifer. *My Sister Rosalind Franklin*. Oxford University Press, 2012. Kindle.

Hager, Thomas. *Force of Nature: The Life of Linus Pauling*. Monroe, 2011. Kindle.

"The Holes in Coal: Research at BCURA and in Paris, 1942–1951." The Rosalind Franklin Papers. National Library of Medicine Profiles in Science. Accessed October 27, 2020. https://profiles.nlm.nih.gov/spotlight/kr/feature/coal.

Holmes, Kenneth C. *Aaron Klug—A Long Way from Durban: A Biography*. Cambridge University Press, 2017. Kindle.

Klug, Aaron. "Rosalind Franklin and the Discovery of the Structure of DNA." *Nature* 219 (August 24, 1968): 808–810. https://doi.org/10.1038/219808a0.

Maddox, Brenda. *Rosalind Franklin: The Dark Lady of DNA*. Harper Perennial, 2013. Kindle.

Markel, Howard. *The Secret of Life: Rosalind Franklin, James Watson, Francis Crick, and the Discovery of DNA's Double Helix*. W. W. Norton, 2021. Kindle.

Olby, Robert C. *The Path to the Double Helix. The Discovery of DNA*. Dover, 1994. Kindle.

"Papers of M H F Wilkins: Draft Text Concerning Wilkins's Reaction to Accusations of Sexism Towards Rosalind Franklin, with Related Papers." K/PP178/6/5/10. Accessed October 27, 2020. Wellcome Collection. https://wellcomelibrary.org/item/b20051360.

Pauling, Linus, and Robert B. Corey. "Compound Helical Configurations of Polypeptide Chains: Structure of Proteins of the α-Keratin Type." *Nature* 171 (January 10, 1953): 59–61. https://doi.org/10.1038/171059a0.

Pauling, Linus, and Robert B. Corey. "Configuration of Polypeptide Chains." *Nature* 168 (September 29, 1951): 550–551. https://doi.org/10.1038/168550a0.

Pauling, Linus, and Robert B. Corey. "A Proposed Structure for the Nucleic Acids." *PNAS*, 39, no. 2 (February 1, 1953): 84–97. https://doi.org/10.1073/pnas.39.2.84.

Pauling, Linus, and Robert B. Corey. "Structure of the Nucleic Acids." *Nature* 171 (February 21, 1953): 346. https://doi.org/10.1038/171346a0.

"The Race for the Double Helix." BBC Internet Archive. Accessed June 20, 2023. https://archive.org/details/TheRacefortheDoubleHelix.

"Reports Etc.—Birkbeck, TMV." FRNK 2/32. Accessed October 27, 2020. Welcome Collection. https://wellcomecollection.org/works/u7bbdfac.

Ridley, Matt. *Francis Crick: Discoverer of the Genetic Code.* HarperCollins, 2012. Kindle.

Sayre, Anne. *Rosalind Franklin and DNA*. W. W. Norton, 1975.

Watson, James D. *The Double Helix: A Personal Account of the Discovery of the Structure of DNA*. Scribner, 2011. Kindle.

Watson, James, and Francis Crick. "Molecular Structure of Nucleic Acids: A Structure for Deoxyribose Nucleic Acid." *Nature* 171 (April 25, 1953): 737–738. https://doi.org/10.1038/171737a0.

Wilkins, Maurice. "Engineering, Biophysics and Physics at King's College, London: New Building." *Nature* 170 (1952): 261–263. https://doi.org/10.1038/170261a0.

Wilkins, Maurice. *The Third Man of the Double Helix: The Autobiography of Maurice Wilkins*. Oxford University Press, 2003. Kindle.

Wilkins, Maurice, A. R. Stokes, and H. R. Wilson. "Molecular Structure of Nucleic Acids: Molecular Structure of Deoxypentose Nucleic Acids." *Nature* 171 (April 25, 1953): 738–740. https://doi.org/10.1038/171738a0.

Index

Photo Acknowledgments

Image credits: Courtesy of Jenifer Glynn via NIH, p. 10; Van de Wiel Photography/Shutterstock, p. 15; Likkii/Shutterstock, p. 16; Science Source, pp. 18, 85; VITTORIO LUZZATI/Science Source, p. 21; National Institutes of Health/Reproduced with permission of Vittorio Luzzati, p. 27; Wikimedia Commons PD, p. 33; King's College London Archives/Science Source, pp. 39, 193; Bettmann Archive/Getty Images, pp. 50, 91, 167, 191, 195, 197; Jpbowen/Wikimedia Commons (CC BY-SA 3.0), p. 53; I.C. Baianu et al/Wikimedia Commons (CC BY-SA 3.0), p. 57; VectorMine/Shutterstock, p. 62; King's College London Archives/Science Source, pp. 65, 194; SSPL/Getty Images, p. 71; Harold Clements/Daily Express/Hulton Archive/Getty Images, pp. 77, 200; National Institutes of Health, p. 93; ttsz/Getty Images, p. 96; Oregon State University/Wikimedia Commons (CC BY-SA 2.0), p. 101; Credit: NANOCLUSTERING/Science Photo Library/ Getty Images, p. 102; Science History Images/Alamy, p. 110; CambridgeNews/Mirrorpixapher/Getty Images, pp. 118, 196; Olena_T/Getty Images, p. 123; Science & Society Picture Library/ SSPL/Getty Images, pp. 126, 198 (top); A. Barrington Brown/Science Source, p. 130; National Institutes of Health/Reproduced with permission of John Finch and the MRCLaboratory of Molecular, p. 137; Camera Press/Alamy, pp. 139, 198 (bottom); Skimage/Alamy, p. 140; Nikolayev Alexey/Shutterstock, p. 145; Photo by Smith Collection/Gado/Getty Images, p. 149 (left); BSIP/UIG/Getty Images, p. 149 (right); Universal History Archive/Universal Images Group via Getty Image, p. 160; Popperfoto/Getty Images, pp. 172, 198; Donaldson Collection/Michael Ochs Archives/Getty Images, p. 178; Cambridge University, p. 187; Universal History Archive/Universal Images Group/Getty Images, p. 201. ATP/RDB/ullstein bild/Getty Images, p. 202. Design element: BeastArt/Shutterstock.

Cover: Universal History Archive/Universal Images Group via Getty Image.

About the Authors

Debbie Loren Dunn is an author of nonfiction books for children and young adults based in Texas. She graduated with a degree in computer science from the University of Texas at Austin and worked in the computer industry for twenty years specializing in databases and data mining. She holds an MFA from Vermont College of Fine Arts and loves true stories about people doing amazing things—especially when others have told them they can't, or they shouldn't. Dunn has served as a board trustee of VCFA, a board member of the Writer's League of Texas, and regional adviser for the SCBWI Austin Chapter. She also served on the board of the ARC—Texas Disability Services and on the board for the Central Texas Crohn's and Colitis Foundation.

Janet Fox is the author of fiction and nonfiction books for young readers. Her work has received numerous awards and accolades including a SCBWI Golden Kite Award, a Bank Street Best Books Award, and the Florida Sunshine State Young Readers Award Master List. Fox received a master of science degree from the University of New York, Albany, in marine geology and authored or coauthored a number of respected scientific research papers. She is a former middle school and high school teacher and has an MFA from Vermont College of Fine Arts. She lives in Bozeman, Montana.